God Bless the
SPECTRUM

Tonight
Clear-Cool

Tomorrow
Sunny

Details on Page 2

PHILADELPHIA DAILY
NEWS

MONDAY, MAY 20, 1974
Our 43d Issue in Our 50th Year

4 ★

15c Sports

God Bless the Flyers!

The City:
3, Fox on 4, McMullen on 32

The Game:
Back Page, 59, 60, 61, 62

God Bless the

SPECTRUM

America's Showplace in Philadelphia: **1967-2009**

Camino Books, Inc.
Philadelphia

God Bless the SPECTRUM

DESIGN DIRECTOR
Kevin Burkett

PHOTO EDITOR
Michael Mercanti

CONTRIBUTING EDITORS
Josh Barnett
Pat McLoone

WRITERS
Ed Barkowitz
Les Bowen
Chuck Darrow
Rich Hofmann
Phil Jasner
Dick Jerardi
Jonathan Takiff

COPY EDITORS
Doug Darroch
Jim DeStefano

PHOTO TECHNICIAN
Rich Bailey

STATISTICS
Bob Vetrone Jr.

PHILADELPHIA
DAILY
NEWS
THE PEOPLE PAPER

Manufactured in the United States of America

1 2 3 4 5 11 10 09

ISBN 978-1-933822-21-1

This book is available at a special discount on bulk purchases for promotional, business, and educational use.

Library of Congress Cataloging-in-Publication Data
God bless the Spectrum: America's showplace in Philadelphia,1967-2009 / by the staff of the Philadelphia daily news.

  p. cm.
  Includes index.
  ISBN 978-1-933822-21-1 (alk. paper)
  1. Spectrum (Arena: Philadelphia, Pa.)–History.
  2. Sports–Pennsylvania–Philadelphia–History.
  I. Philadelphia daily news (Philadelphia, Pa.: 1925)
  II. Title.

GV416.P (Philadelphia, Pa.)+
725'.80974811–dc22   2009011187

Camino Books, Inc.
P.O. Box 59026
Philadelphia, PA 19102
www.caminobooks.com

Photo illustration by KEVIN BURKETT

Welcome to the SPECTRUM

LOOKING THROUGH THE PAGES of this amazing book brings back a flood of emotions and personal memories of a wonderful place. The Spectrum is and always will be my baby. The Spectrum's opening marked the creation of a new destination in South Philadelphia. It was built primarily to accommodate the birth of the Philadelphia Flyers. It became a great home for them, as well as for the Philadelphia 76ers, and made South Broad Street a true mecca for sports and entertainment.

In addition to being a spectacular venue to watch the Flyers and Sixers, it became "The House That Rock Built," as nearly every major artist performed live in the Spectrum. It hosted one of Elvis Presley's final concerts, shows by Bruce Springsteen, Billy Joel and Frank Sinatra, and an incredible 53 performances by the Grateful Dead. The other legends who appeared are way too many to mention here.

The Spectrum became a special place for millions of fans throughout the Greater Philadelphia Region, hosting hundreds of events each year. Some may forget many of the unusual events we hosted, including field and track, roller derby, professional wrestling, rodeo, ballet, opera and so much more. We literally blew the roof off the Spectrum! And that happened, too.

As I read through this book, the memories keep coming back to me. Who could ever forget the day the Flyers won their first Stanley Cup on May 19, 1974? I can still hear the roar of that crowd as the clock wound down with Joe Watson standing behind Bernie Parent, looking up at the scoreboard as time expired. I can still remember that collective breath everyone held as Christian Laettner took that jump shot in overtime to put Duke in the 1992 Final Four. I'll also never forget the game on Jan. 11, 1976, in which our Philadelphia Flyers faced off against a Russian Army team that was known as "the best team in the world," and watching in disbelief as the Russians left the ice midway through the first period in what would be a precursor to their resounding defeat.

I'd like to personally thank all of our employees through the years for their dedication, enthusiasm and creativity in helping us make the Spectrum so special. Numerous employees started with us at the Spectrum and continue to work with us at the Wachovia Center.

My children grew up in the Spectrum, watching events and playing in the hallways. When the wrecking ball takes away the bricks and mortar of the Spectrum, we will always have the many wonderful memories of America's Showplace.

Thank you, Philadelphia, for sharing these many memories with us. You, the fans, are the reason the Spectrum is and always will be special for me.

Chairman, Comcast-Spectacor

Laying the
groundwork
in 1966.

CHAPTER ONE

Building
History

The man whose vision became
the Spectrum revisits the memories
that will outlast the building.

By Rich Hofmann

ARK THE CAR, walk in the back door, past the guard, "Good morning, sir," up the stairs, one carpeted flight, into the Spectrum concourse. It is the house where Ed Snider grew up and he looks at it with that eye, and mind's eye. "I'm almost never over here anymore," he says, and his head is kind of swiveling as he says it, a quick panorama to catch the little details.

The owner's box is maybe 50 feet away. It is from there that Snider presided — and that is the right word, presided. His guests learned quickly not to bother the man while a Flyers game was being played. If they were losing, his stare could be chilling. As he says, "I'm intense. I'm watching the game. I'll socialize between periods, depending on the score."

The box is set right among the fans in the lower level. From Snider's seat in the front row on the end, he could and did talk to the patrons. He did not always set a good example for group behavior. "We eventually had to put glass in because I was interacting too much," he says. "I would be standing on the ledge here, yelling about something, getting the crowd all riled up. One time I ran all the way down to the glass and started gesturing at the official. Cost me five grand."

Every longtime Snider watcher knew about the phone at Snider's seat, a phone that went through several incarnations over the years. From the press box across the way, a common sight following a controversial whistle was to see Snider pick up the phone and then to see the general manager of the day — Keith Allen, Bob Clarke, whoever — pick up his phone in the press box and listen to the boss rant.

One time, after a big fight, the referee was reciting

Snow and ice obviously didn't slow construction, which took just 15 months. TONY GARGANO

the penalties to the timekeeper and the public-address announcer, Lou Nolan. Snider called down to Nolan and said, "What the hell is going on?" Nolan then put the phone down for a minute to find out. When the referee was done, Nolan picked it up. Snider was mad. Nolan explained he needed to get the information from the referee. Snider said, "Look, when I call, you put the referee on hold."

Snider laughs now as he tells the story. He is nostalgic, sitting in his old box, walking around his old home. This is where Ed Snider became Ed Snider and he knows it. He was there for the birth of the Flyers and the building in 1967. It was from here that he built the first tiny studio for PRISM, the cable-television network. It was here where he learned the arena-management business that is a core piece of his business empire. It was here where he realized one day that renovations would not solve the modern sports

revenue conundrum, and began planning for the Wachovia Center across the parking lot.

It was here at the Spectrum, which might very well have been the first arena in the country not named after a war or a hero or a politician or a donor or a team or the owner of the joint. Spectrum. "I think it was Stan Hochman in the *Daily News* who said it sounded like a medical instrument," Snider says.

You walk around and the journey triggers decades of memories. Snider searches around, getting somebody to unlock a series of doors, trying to find the little room where he and some NHL officials huddled after the Russians walked off the ice. They came back after Snider asked the question that provided the answer: "Have they been paid yet?"

Down the hall is the gate that now divides the hallways between the home and visiting dressing room. "Homer's Gate," Snider says, recalling the fight

When the Spectrum was built, JFK Stadium was the only other sports facility in the neighborhood.
Temple University Libraries Urban Archives

Originally constructed as a double-decker, popular demand led to the addition of a third seating level in 1972.

between Paul Holmgren and Wayne Cashman that prompted its construction. Except Snider has some of the details wrong, so he picks up the phone and calls Holmgren, his traveling general manager, to get them straight. "What, are you going to make me pay for it now?" Holmgren asks, and Snider's laughter fills the hallway. "Must be a slow day up there."

It is slow. Snider is in no hurry as we poke around. The building has meant a lot of things to a lot of people — Sixers, concerts, wrestling, whatnot — but as we enter the Flyers' old dressing room, well, this is the place. There was never any doubt about that. The Phantoms use it now, but Snider can still see things. He says he can see a Stanley Cup celebration. He says he can see the game after goaltender Pelle Lindbergh died.

He looks at a soda cooler. "We didn't have Pepsi," he says. "Back then, all they drank was beer. They sat on their stools and smoked cigarettes between periods. My God, the world has changed.

"When I walk in this locker room, I mostly think of the happy days. I remember celebrations and giant wins, winning the conference, winning the Stanley Cup, all of the great things we went through."

Outside in the red seats, so many stories were told. The Cups were won. The roof blew off. An entire style of play, loved and loathed, was transformed into a franchise's identity.

The Spectrum's proud papa, Ed Snider, walks its halls in its final year. DAVID MAIALETTI / Daily News

15

"I don't know if I'm smart enough to know, but I think the building had to contribute to our success," Snider says. "The crowd was such a big factor. People didn't want to come play us here — remember 'the Philly flu?' If we were in the Wachovia Center and the rules were still the same as they were back in those days, it would still be a scary place to play. But the more the atmosphere was intimidating, the more it added — icing on the cake."

He stops for a second.

"I really miss my interaction with the fans," he says. "I still have some, and they're great to me, and I feel privileged because of that. But it's nothing like the interaction I had when we were here.

"People ask my about my emotions. My emotions are not tied into the physical plant — they're tied to the memories, to what went on here. I'm rarely over here ... and I don't walk over here and cry and get all emotional now that the building is going to be torn down. I get sad thinking about it, but that isn't the dominant emotion.

"Because I will always, always, have all the memories. I don't have to walk into the building itself to have those memories." S

Above, Howard Baldwin, who later became a Pittsburgh Penguins owner, works the box office. At left, fans line up for a game in 1969.

The Name

The new arena planned for Broad and Pattison was going to be "the first in the country that didn't have a dead person's name or a war connotation," Lou Scheinfeld says, looking back from the final days of the building he had helped name, more than 40 years earlier.

Scheinfeld, a vice president of the company building the new arena, was tromping around the muddy foundation one day with Bill Becker, who had been involved with the Flyers' uniform and logo designs. They were wearing boots and hard hats and throwing out terms they thought might fit.

"Splendid, spectacular — then the word 'spectrum' popped up," Scheinfeld recalls. He isn't sure which of them said it, but he remembers they weren't sure what it meant. When they looked it up, they saw something about "a series of colorful images" formed by light moving through a prism. When they thought about the variety of events planned for their arena, they thought they had nailed it.

When they brought their idea back to the people in charge, there were murmurs about evoking an image of a medical instrument (a speculum). Another arena official was keen on the idea of "The Keystone Arena," or simply "The Keystone."

Scheinfeld says they formed a presentation that might have been "a little heavyhanded." Becker's Spectrum logo was modern and colorful; the "Keystone" logo was modeled on the image posted on gas pumps in Pennsylvania to signify they had passed inspection. Scheinfeld also discovered something like 60 businesses

Letter by Letter

According to Ed Snider and Lou Scheinfeld, the letters that spell SPECTRUM stand for:

SP Sports and South Philadelphia
E Entertainment
C Circuses and Concerts
T Theatrics
R Recreation
UM stadiUM and auditoriUM
(and according to Lou Scheinfeld: "Um, isn't this place spectacular?"

in the Philadelphia area that used "Keystone" as part of their name, including exterminators and dry cleaners.

Scheinfeld remembers the group being persuaded, but the "Keystone" guy insisting they take a larger sampling. So through Ed Snider, one of the principals in the effort and an Eagles vice president, they arranged to present the names to the Eagles' office staff. "The vote was 30-1" in favor of The Spectrum, Scheinfeld says.

When the name was unveiled and its logic explained, not all skepticism vanished.

"It sounds like they've reached too far in groping for something unique," Stan Hochman wrote in the *Daily News*. "There are no Orangutan Dry Cleaners in the phone book, either, and orangutans are big and bold and colorful."

— *Les Bowen*

1976: A Full Spectrum

The Bicentennial celebration helps bring in some star-studded events.

BERNIE MOSER

Jan. 11: Flyers vs. Soviet Red Army

In more ways than one, the two-time defending Stanley Cup champion Flyers beat the Soviet Red Army team, 4-1. The Russians leave the ice at one point because of the rough play. They return, but the thumping continues. That evening, the Sixers beat the visiting Green Army (Boston Celtics), 118-107.

Jan. 13: Watts Beats Hagler

A 22-year-old middleweight by the name of Marvin Hagler (25-0-1 entering the bout) loses a disputed majority decision to Bobby "Boogaloo" Watts in a 10-round bout. Hagler's second defeat would also come at the Spectrum less than 2 months later (March 9) when he lost another 10-round decision to Willie "The Worm" Monroe.

▲ Jan. 20: NHL All-Star Game

Montreal's Pete Mahovlich has a goal and three assists to lead the Wales Conference to a 7-5 victory over the Flyers' Campbell Conference.

Feb. 3: NBA All-Star Game

The Washington Bullets' Dave Bing, then 32, shows the youngsters how it's done with 16 points and four assists to lead the East to a 123-109 victory. The Sixers' Doug Collins has 12 points and George McGinnis 10. The Lakers' Kareem Abdul-Jabbar has 22 points and 15 rebounds for the West.

March 27 & 29: NCAA Final Four

The Big Ten takes over South Philadelphia at the Final Four. In the semifinals, Michigan disposes of undefeated Rutgers and Indiana deals UCLA just its third tournament loss since 1963. Bobby Knight's Hoosiers then methodically take apart the Wolverines in the championship game to cap a perfect season.

May 13 & 16: Stanley Cup Finals

The two-time defending Stanley Cup champion Flyers bring the finals back to the Spectrum, but are unable to stop the Montreal Canadiens, who win Games 3 and 4 to complete a sweep for their first of four consecutive Cups.

June 28: Elvis is in the Building

The fourth of five shows Elvis Presley would perform at the Spectrum in his career.

Oct. 22: The Doctor is in the House

Julius Erving makes his NBA, Sixers and Spectrum debut, having been acquired two days before from the New Jersey Nets. The Sixers lose to the Spurs, 121-118, but a new era has begun.

▼ Oct. 25 & 27: Bruce Springsteen

Following a disappointing Spectrum debut in 1973 (opening for Chicago), Bruce Springsteen & the E Street Band return for two dynamic shows.

— *Bob Vetrone Jr.*

ELWOOD P. SMITH / Daily News

Just another day at the office for the Broad Street Bullies, seen here mixing it up with the California Seals in December 1973. Inquirer archives

Bobby Clarke and Bernie Parent after the Flyers' first Stanley Cup championship.
BERNIE MOSER

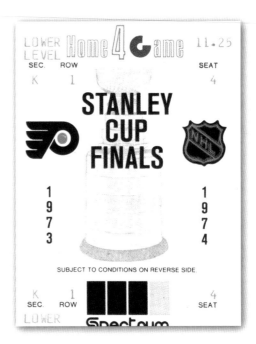

CHAPTER TWO

The Flyers

In a city where you couldn't buy a puck, the Broad Street Bullies hooked us early and haven't let go.

By Les Bowen

T SEEMS STRANGE THAT IN A TOWN that values history so much, in the American city that has preserved more of this nation's roots than any other, the building where the Flyers won their first Stanley Cup is about to become nothing but memories and a plaque.

Very soon, you will not be able to see the spot at center ice where Kate Smith stood to belt out "God Bless America," or the perch from which Gene Hart crowed, "The Flyers win the Stanley Cup! The Flyers win the Stanley Cup!"

The birth of the Flyers, in a city that lacked a rich history with the sport, where original Flyers coach Keith Allen has remarked that you couldn't buy a hockey puck back in the mid-'60s, was tied to the birth of the Spectrum. The city already had the Sixers, the NBA franchise that arrived from Syracuse

DUFOR STUDIO

Flanked by Penguins captain Ab McDonald and Flyers captain Lou Angotti, NHL president Clarence Campbell drops the ceremonial first puck before the Spectrum's first NHL game, Oct. 19, 1967. Plenty of good seats were still available (left). Spectrum archives

in the wake of the Warriors' departure. But building a privately financed arena, across the street from where Veterans Stadium already was being planned, was contingent on Philadelphia getting one of a half-dozen expansion franchises the NHL was handing out in 1966 as it proposed to double in size.

The group applying for the hockey franchise, which included Eagles minority owner Ed Snider, had to build the arena in order to qualify. It tiptoed through the early stages of negotiation with the city, not wanting to encourage competition from other groups that might have the same idea; the NHL's proposed expansion didn't seem to be on Philadelphia's civic radar, and Snider's group wanted it to stay that way.

It got the OK from the NHL on Feb. 9, 1966, and broke ground on the Spectrum less than 4 months later, June 1. The new team was to begin play in September 1967.

The early days weren't easy. The advance season-ticket sale, as local newspapers ran articles educating fans about the rules of hockey, was 2,100. The home opener, Oct. 19 against Pittsburgh, came after the Flyers got off to a 1-2 start on the road, only the last of those games even being televised back home. Opening Night attendance of 7,812 was about 800 short of what management needed to average to break even. Hart, then the public-address announcer, repeatedly explained icing and offside whistles. But the Flyers won, 1-0.

The Spectrum's surprise sun roof (left) forced the Flyers and Sixers to relocate for the last couple months of their 1967-68 seasons, and left fans frustrated. Spectrum archives

It helped that the six new expansion teams were clustered in one division; the Flyers experienced some early success (they would win the new division), and crowds grew, at least until Feb. 17, 1968, when portions of the roof blew away before an Ice Capades performance. Temporary repairs were made, but a March 1 storm caused a much bigger roof rift. The Flyers finished their inaugural season in Quebec City, though they were able to return home for their first playoff series, which they lost to St. Louis in seven games.

Hard to believe now that it was just 6 years after that first playoff experience that Joe Watson was skating up to the puck behind Bernie Parent's net, waiting for the final seconds to tick away on the Boston Bruins, signaling the first Stanley Cup championship ever won by an expansion team. That came just a year after the Flyers finally won a playoff series for the first time, a victory set up by Gary Dornhoefer's acrobatic overtime goal in Game 5 against Minnesota

and goalie Cesare Maniago. Dornhoefer's flight was commemorated in a statue outside the Spectrum.

For a few years there, it looked as if every Broad Street Bully might end up with his own statue. Seldom has a franchise and a fan base ever bonded the way Philadelphia and coach Fred Shero's Flyers did. There could never be a better exemplification of Philly's scrappy, hard-working, "Rocky"-like spirit than the Bobby Clarke-led teams that invented the victory parade down Broad Street. They remain the gold standard of fan devotion; if any of them has had to buy his own drink in a Delaware Valley bar in the intervening 35 years, the place must have been full of out-of-towners that night, attending a convention or something.

On May 19, 1974, Kate Smith sang her song live in front of 17,007, many of whom still treasure the ticket stubs. Rick MacLeish scored the only goal of a 1-0 Game 6 win that made Philadelphia a hockey town, perhaps forever. "Miracle Flyers Take the Cup And City Goes Wild With Joy," said the *Inquirer* headline.

Gary Dornhoefer beats Minnesota North Stars goalie Cesare Maniago for the Flyers' first-ever overtime goal in Game 5 of the playoff quarterfinals in 1973. Below, young fans climb the statue commemorating the play. Spectrum archives

Their clinching win the next year came in Buffalo, so '74 was the Spectrum's only dance with the big silver trophy, though the Flyers made the finals again in '76, '80, '85 and '87, before moving to their new home following the 1995-96 season.

The Spectrum saw the Flyers defeat the Central Red Army team, with the whole continent cheering, on Jan. 11, 1976. It saw them skate through a 35-game unbeaten streak in 1979-80. On Nov. 14, 1985, it mourned the car-crash death of Vezina Trophy-winning goalie Pelle Lindbergh, the memorial held before a 5-3 victory over Edmonton, played with the boards cleansed of advertising. On Dec. 8, 1987, the Spectrum was the venue where Ron Hextall became the first NHL goaltender to shoot the puck into the other team's net.

You could say the beginning of the end for the Spectrum as the Flyers' home came on Oct. 10, 1992. That was when Eric Lindros played his first home game, electrifying the crowd by stepping over New Jersey goalie Chris Terreri's pokecheck to score the game-winner.

Flyers Records: 1967-1996

	Championship season											

	Complete Season					At the Spectrum					
	Regular Season			Playoffs		Regular Season			Playoffs	
Season	W	L	T	W	L	W	L	T	W	L
1967-68	31	32	11	3	4	14	11	5	2	2
1968-69	20	35	21	0	4	14	16	8	0	2
1969-70	17	35	21	—	—	11	14	13	—	—
1970-71	28	33	17	0	4	20	10	9	0	2
1971-72	26	38	14	—	—	19	13	7	—	—
1972-73	37	30	11	5	6	27	8	4	2	3
1973-74	50	16	12	12	5	28	6	5	9	0
1974-75	51	18	11	12	5	32	6	2	8	1
1975-76	51	13	16	8	8	36	2	2	6	3
1976-77	48	16	16	4	6	33	6	1	1	4
1977-78	45	20	15	7	5	29	6	5	5	1
1978-79	40	25	15	3	5	26	10	4	2	3
1979-80	48	12	20	13	6	27	5	8	9	2
1980-81	41	24	15	6	6	23	9	8	5	2
1981-82	38	31	11	1	3	25	10	5	0	2
1982-83	49	23	8	0	3	29	8	3	0	2
1983-84	44	26	10	0	3	25	10	5	0	1
1984-85	53	20	7	12	7	32	4	4	8	2
1985-86	53	23	4	2	3	33	6	1	1	2
1986-87	46	26	8	15	11	29	9	2	7	6
1987-88	38	33	9	3	4	20	14	6	2	1
1988-89	36	36	8	10	9	22	15	3	4	5
1989-90	30	39	11	—	—	17	19	4	—	—
1990-91	33	37	10	—	—	18	16	6	—	—
1991-92	32	37	11	—	—	22	11	7	—	—
1992-93	36	37	11	—	—	23	14	4	—	—
1993-94	35	39	10	—	—	19	19	3	—	—
1994-95	28	16	4	10	5	16	7	1	5	3
1995-96	45	24	13	6	6	27	9	5	3	3
Totals	**1,129**	**794**	**350**	**132**	**118**	**696**	**293**	**140**	**79**	**52**

These Flyers fans are forces of habit. ELWOOD P. SMITH / Daily News

Fans had a Stanley Cup to get excited about in 1975, too.

By the Numbers
At the Spectrum

Games	1,260
Wins	775
Losses	345
Ties	140
Winning Percentage	.671
Goals For	4,845
Goals Against	3,396
Attendance	20,698,158

All numbers include regular-season and playoff games

The historic trade that brought Lindros' rights to Philadelphia came at a ruinous price — six players, including Peter Forsberg, $15 million and two first-round draft choices. But what the Lindros deal did was help get the new building built. The current Sixers and Flyers home, first known as the CoreStates Center, now the Wachovia Center, was on the drawing board for several years before Snider pulled together the financing package and sold the luxury boxes that would ensure success. Trading for Lindros, who seemed destined to become the game's best player, was the catalyst that eventually helped bring all that together, 2 years after he arrived.

Eric Lindros and Bobby Clarke, together on ice.

GEORGE REYNOLDS / Daily News

It was fitting, then, that in the final Flyers regular-season game played at the Spectrum, April 11, 1996, the closing ceremony included victory laps by players from previous eras and from that team. Lindros and Clarke, then the GM, took their lap as a pair. They would part bitterly 5 years later, but on that night, in that building, they stood together — the captain who "made" the Spectrum and the captain who "made" the new building.

Like the building itself, their partnership proved temporary. S

The playing of Kate Smith's 'God Bless America' led to four live performances by the Flyers' good-luck charm. Said Kate, blissfully ignoring the Broad Street Bullies' reputation: 'What could be better than being linked with something so wholesome as good, clean sport?' Spectrum archives

When Kate Sings

The Flyers win 76 percent of the time when Kate Smith's 'God Bless America' substitutes for the national anthem.

Season	W	L	T	Season	W	L	T
1969-70	7	1	1	1989-90	1	0	0
1970-71	4	0	0	1990-91	1	1	0
1971-72	8	0	0	1991-92	1	0	0
1972-73	10	2	0	1992-93	1	0	0
1973-74	8	0	0	1993-94	1	2	0
1974-75	6	0	0	1994-95	0	0	0
1975-76	4	2	0	1995-96	1	0	0
1976-77	2	1	0	1996-97	0	0	0
1977-78	1	0	1	1997-98	0	0	0
1978-79	2	2	0	1998-99	0	0	0
1979-80	0	0	0	1999-00	0	0	0
1980-81	1	1	0	2000-01	0	0	0
1981-82	1	0	0	2001-02	2	0	0
1982-83	0	0	0	2002-03	0	2	0
1983-84	0	0	0	2003-04	0	0	0
1984-85	1	0	0	2005-06	2	1	0
1985-86	0	0	0	2006-07	0	0	1
1986-87	3	0	0	2007-08	7	2	0
1987-88	0	1	1	2008-09	1	0	0
1988-89	0	2	0	Total	76	20	4

SOURCE: www.flyershistory.net

Ed Snider does the honors of filling the Cup during the 1974 celebration. RICHARD TITLEY / Inquirer

Don Saleski (left) and Bobby Clarke join the entire city in erupting as the first Stanley Cup is won. RUSTY KENNEDY / AP

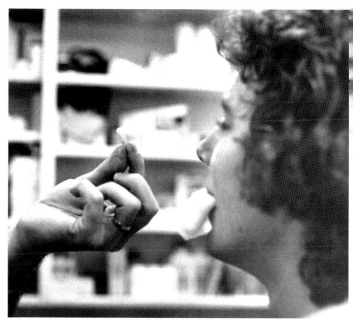

Bobby Clarke doesn't need a mirror to see his tooth now. BERNIE MOSER

Reggie Leach reacts to one of his five goals against the Bruins on May 6, 1976 (above). In the locker room, he poses with the game puck.
Spectrum archives

It was quite nice, indeed, when the Flyers repeated as Stanley Cup champions and paraded past Billy Penn and 2.3 million delirious fans. SAM PSORAS / Daily News

Flyers fans react to a goal during the NHL-record 35-game unbeaten streak (25-0-10) in 1979-80. E.W. FAIRCLOTH / Daily News

Coach Pat Quinn oversees the Nov. 27 win over Hartford. ELWOOD P. SMITH / Daily News

Bobby Clarke rubs elbows with 51-year-old Gordie Howe during one of two wins over Hartford Whalers during the streak.

GEORGE REYNOLDS / Daily News

Ron Hextall becomes the first NHL goalie to shoot a puck into the opposing net against visiting Bruins, Dec. 8, 1987.

The ultimately frustrating Eric Lindros era was not without its good times. Here is Lindros flanked by his Legion of Doom linemates, Mikael Renberg (left) and John LeClair.
STEVEN M. FALK / Daily News

Flyers celebrate J.J. Daigneault's goal at 14:28 of the third period that won Game 6 of the 1987 Stanley Cup finals against Edmonton, 3-2. GEORGE REYNOLDS / Daily News

Flyers legends reunite at the Spectrum before a 2008 preseason game against the Phantoms. STEVEN M. FALK / Daily News

At far left, longtime Flyers broadcaster Gene Hart shares the booth with defenseman Moose Dupont. At right is PA announcer Lou Nolan. Spectrum archives

Bernie Parent faces a two-on-none break. Spectrum archives

Flyers' Wives Fight for Lives Carnival

It is not an exaggeration to call the Flyers' Wives Fight
for Lives Carnival the model of charity fund-raising for
sports teams. The annual Sunday-afternoon event offers
fans the chance to have their photo taken with their favorite
Flyers, get autographs, take a shot on goal, take aim at a
dunk tank, play spin-a-wheel and other such family-friendly
activities, as well as bid on auction items. It began in 1977
to benefit a cancer center at Hahnemann University Hospital
and took on new meaning a few months later when leukemia
claimed the life of former Flyers defenseman Barry Ashbee.
The Barry Ashbee Research Laboratory at Hahnemann
was the largest recipient of funds from the carnival,
but more than 100 other charities have benefited from
the more than $21 million that has been raised by the team's
hard-working wives.

Spectrum archives

ED MAHAN

ED MAHAN

Pelle Lindbergh is one of the great tragic figures in Flyers history. The Swedish goalie broke in with the Flyers in 1981-82, and won the Vezina Trophy in 1984-85. He died in a car crash in November 1985, and the Flyers held an emotional tribute before the next home game. ED MAHAN

Barry Ashbee (top) was the first Flyer to have his number retired, followed by Bernie Parent, Bobby Clarke and Bill Barber (below). Spectrum archives

Retired Numbers

BARRY ASHBEE
4

- Defenseman known for dedication and tenacity
- Led Flyers' first Stanley Cup team in plus-minus with plus-53, sustained career-ending eye injury in semifinals
- Became assistant coach, died of leukemia in 1977

BERNIE PARENT
1

- Goalie acquired from Boston, traded, then reacquired
- Won Vezina and Conn Smythe trophies in 1974 & '75 as league's top goalie and playoff MVP
- Record: 232-141-103, 50 shutouts
- Hockey Hall of Fame (1984)

BOBBY CLARKE
16

- Heart and soul of 1974 & '75 Stanley Cup champs
- Despite diabetes, had 358 goals, 852 assists and three Hart Trophies (MVP in 1973, '75 & '76) in 15 seasons
- Former GM, now senior VP
- Hockey Hall of Fame (1987)

BILL BARBER
7

- Natural center moved to left wing on Bobby Clarke's line
- Had five 40-goal seasons (50 in 1975-76)
- Calder Cup-winning coach with Phantoms, later coached Flyers
- Hockey Hall of Fame (1990)

JUANA ANDERSON / Daily News

The **Red Army** Game

Moose Dupont intervenes as Dave Schultz introduces himself to the Russians. Spectrum archives

THE MOST INFAMOUS WALKOUT in the history of hockey happened on Jan. 11, 1976, in front of a jeering, sellout Spectrum crowd.

This was the time of the Cold War, before there were Russian players in the NHL. The hard-fought Summit Series, which Canada won by a 4-3-1 margin in 1972, had raised fears that the brand of hockey played by the mysterious Soviets was actually superior to that played in the NHL.

The Central Red Army Team's 1975-76 four-game tour, the next encounter between East and West, was doing nothing to allay those fears. The Soviets beat the Rangers and the Bruins and tied the Canadiens. For the finale, the Flyers, defending two-time Stanley Cup champions, carried onto their home ice the honor of a league that in other circumstances looked down its nose at their brawling, lunchpail style.

A couple of hard, clean, Flyers-style hits ruffled Russian feathers. Then Ed Van Impe, a dependable antagonist, came out of the penalty

Ed Van Impe lays out Russian star Valeri Kharlamov with an unpenalized elbow that led to the walkout. Spectrum archives

A Flyers fixture since 1972, Dave 'Sign Man' Leonardi came prepared for the Russians.

Red Army goalie
Vladislav Tretiak
takes a nap.

Spectrum archives

box and nailed Red Army star Valeri Kharlamov with an unpenalized elbow to the face. Coach Konstantin Loktev took his time sending out the next shift, waving at the referee, dramatizing his plight. The ref, Lloyd Gilmour, penalized the Red Army for delay.

That was enough for Loktev, who waved his players to the locker room 11 minutes, 21 seconds into the first period of a 0-0 game. Immediately, an old-fashioned Cold War summit was convened, an NHL delegation comprising league president Clarence Campbell, players association director Alan Eagleson and Flyers chairman Ed Snider meeting with Russian officials, including Soviet hockey federation head Vyacheslav Koloskov, while fans waited and rumors swirled.

Legends differ on what happened to get the Russians back on the ice, after a 17-minute delay. Campbell later emphasized that Koloskov agreed when Campbell said it would be an international disaster for such a series to end this way. But the Philadelphia version — endorsed by Snider in the 1996 Flyers history "Full Spectrum" — holds that the blunt-speaking team chairman pointed out that the Red Army group hadn't yet been paid, and would not be, if it refused to return to the ice.

The Russians returned, and 17 seconds later, Reggie Leach tipped home a Bill Barber shot for a 1-0 Flyers lead.

The Spectrum went crazy.

As the first period wound down, Gary Dornhoefer picked off a defender, sending Rick MacLeish in alone on Vladislav Tretiak. MacLeish beat Tretiak's glove for a 2-0 Flyers lead.

Later, Joe Watson scored shorthanded, making it 3-0 before the Army got on the board, but not really back into the game. Larry Goodenough's third-period goal set the 4-1 final score. Flyers coach Fred Shero joked that Watson, not a noted scorer, beating Tretiak shorthanded set back Soviet hockey 25 years.

The Flyers had absolutely destroyed the feared

big red machine, ringing up a 49-13 shots advantage against a clearly intimidated group. Loktev complained that the hosts played "like animals."

Nobody apologized. It's hard to explain, today, the importance of such a victory, achieved in such a way, against such a hated opponent. Many years later, in far-flung cities, people traveling with the Flyers would often hear from desk clerks, waiters, reporters and random fans of the sport, who would venture the same grudging endorsement. "I always hated the Broad Street Bullies," they would begin. "But when they beat the Red Army Team … !"

When they beat the Red Army Team, suddenly their style seemed so much less repugnant.

The Soviet Union is long gone now, and now the Spectrum is joining it.

— Les Bowen

A Russian newspaper printed this editorial cartoon as part of its coverage of the game, depicting the Flyers as club-wielding thugs.

Above, diplomacy takes a back seat as the Russians delay the game after Ed Van Impe's hit before leaving for the locker room. Afterward, the Flyers shake the hands of the conquered enemy.

Spectrum archives

Charles Barkley
takes to the air.
JERRY LODRIGUSS /
Inquirer

The joint is jumpin' during this win over the Lakers in Game 5 of the 1982 NBA Finals.
DICK BELL / Inquirer

CHAPTER THREE

The
Sixers

It became the Doctor's office in 1976, and the patients' patience was rewarded with an NBA title in 1983.

By Phil Jasner

G ROWING UP IN LEEDS, Ala., following the NBA on TV, Charles Barkley said he basically knew about four major arenas:

Madison Square Garden in New York, the Forum in Los Angeles, the Boston Garden ...

And the Spectrum, the building that would house the 76ers for the first eight seasons of what would become his Hall of Fame career.

"That was all I knew about, those arenas, those teams," Barkley says. "When I got there, Moses Malone dressed on one side of the locker room, Julius Erving on the other side. The locker room was so small, if you turned your head around too fast you'd kiss somebody.

"There was the passion of the fans. Sometimes they'd go overboard, but they really cared. All they wanted to do was win. To go out on the court, you had to go down a runway, through the fans, high-fiving them all the way out. It

Doctor J
operates on
Dave Cowens.
PRENTICE COLE /
Daily News

was our home court. When we won, it was heaven. When we lost, it was hell."

The building, at one time or another, also was home to Naismith Basketball Hall of Famers Alex Hannum, Wilt Chamberlain, Hal Greer, Chuck Daly, Jack Ramsay, Malone ...

And Doctor J.

The Sixers made their debut in the building Oct. 18, 1967. The Doctor arrived Oct. 22, 1976, to begin an 11-season journey that included three trips to the Finals before winning a championship, sweeping the Lakers in 1983.

But not even Doc could possibly have been ready for what awaited him before he ever played a minute.

That was an impetuous, dedicated, probably overcaffeinated season ticketholder named Steve Solms.

As legendary public-address announcer Dave Zinkoff introduced Erving, the incandescent star of the defunct ABA who had just been acquired from the New York Nets in a landmark deal, Solms raced from his sidecourt seat to the line of uniformed Sixers standing on the court. He handed the startled Erving a medical bag inscribed with Erving's initials.

"I remember when his name was announced," Solms says, "I said, 'Do I have the guts to do this?' I said, 'I do.' And I did. When I got to him, I said, 'Don't be nervous. It's just a doctor's bag.' He looked at me like I was nuts. I told him to raise it up and the crowd would go nuts. He did. They did."

Pro basketball fans in Philadelphia had begun following their teams in the Broadwood Hotel, where a dance, complete with a full-scale orchestra, followed each game. They went from there to the Arena, then to Convention Hall. The Spectrum, though, was state of the art for its time. To the players, to the fans, it somehow had a heartbeat.

"It was a place where I had such beautiful memories, such joy, so much pleasure," Solms says. "It was a great building, very intimate, with more warmth. It

Zink's Legacy

ELWOOD P. SMITH / Daily News

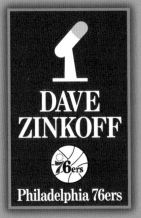

1 DAVE ZINKOFF 76ers Philadelphia 76ers

It would not be a stretch to say Dave Zinkoff holds the record for more performances at the Spectrum, since he was as much entertainer as public-address announcer. His dry wit and intonations made him so much a part of the spectacle that he is the only non-player from the Sixers to have a banner in the rafters of the Wachovia Center. Zink was the voice of Philly pro basketball from 1946 with the Warriors (he worked Wilt CHAAAM-berlain's 100-point game in 1962 in Hershey) until his death in 1985. His showmanship was encouraged by Harlem Globetrotters owner Abe Saperstein when Zink served as the team's announcer (Zinkoff even wrote a book about their first world tour in 1952). A Temple alum, he also worked Owls events, A's and Phillies games at Shibe Park, and boxing and wrestling shows at Convention Hall. He also was an Army veteran and brought countless amateur boxing shows to veterans centers.

Zinkisms

❝There is no smoking in the seating area. If you must smoke, please do not exhale. ❞

❝Would the woman sitting in section T, row one, seat four, please remove your sweater ... from the railing. ❞

was a jewel. It fit just right in the city."

Still, Pat Williams' vivid memories tell him that the then-owner of the Sixers, Irv Kosloff, was reluctant to leave Convention Hall.

"It wasn't an automatic with him," says Williams, who became the Sixers' general manager. "He had grave reservations. He loved the intimacy of Convention Hall. He grew up there. He really had to be sold on the move.

"The first year there, the roof blew off. Bob Vetrone, who had covered basketball for the old *Bulletin*, was working for the team by then. We had to move to the Palestra, and Bob said: 'I don't know quite how to act. We're just not used to having a roof over our heads.' "

This was before the era of the Internet, before cable TV, before the time of instant information. This was where a part-time, game-night employee, working full-time for a record company, prevailed on Williams

to allow a young singer to have his new song played on the arena system. Williams grudgingly agreed.

The singer was Barry Manilow. The song was "Mandy." Within weeks, Manilow and "Mandy" were at the top of the charts.

It was a venue in which, if you weren't already famous, you could become famous on some level.

It was where Willie Burton, a journeyman forward recently acquired on waivers with a history of battling personal demons, somehow one-upped Michael Jordan. Dec. 13, 1994: Burton torched the Miami Heat for 53 points, breaking the floor record of 52 established by the Chicago Bulls superstar. There were fans who insisted Burton seemed to be talking to the basketball as he warmed up.

"I do that all the time," Burton said. "That's just me."

No one ever broke his record.

It was the place where Barkley, on Feb. 20, 1985, his 22nd birthday, raised up for a two-handed slam

dunk at the east end, swung on the rim and moved the 2,240-pound basket support about 6 inches to the right.

"The last time that support was moved," said then-Spectrum publicist Larry Rubin, "it was by a forklift."

There are expensive seats next to the team benches in just about all the new arenas. Those seats, albeit slightly less pricey, were there in the Spectrum, too. But there was more to those grand, old seats than simply the view or the prestige.

"We used to get food for Charles and Rick Mahorn," says longtime season ticketholder Bryan Abrams. "We'd keep it underneath. They'd go for it when the coaches weren't looking."

The Spectrum was the place where, in the Lakers' regular-season visit in 1982-83, Erving threw down what became an immortalized fastbreak dunk described by Lakers announcer Chick Hearn as "Rock the baby to sleep."

Above: On Easter Sunday in 1981, just 6,704 paid to see the Sixers beat the Bucks in Game 7 of the Eastern Conference semifinals. BOB SACHA / Inquirer

76ERS By the Numbers
■ ■■ ■ At the Spectrum ■ ■■ ■

Games	**1,241**
Wins	**805**
Losses	**436**
Winning Percentage	**.649**
Points Scored	**136,652**
Opponents' Points	**131,830**
Attendance	**15,138,099**

All numbers include regular-season and playoff games
Includes game of March 13, 2009

SPORTS RADIO-WCAU 121

Wilt Chamberlain shoots over the Celtics' Wayne Embry in 1967-68, the only season the Spectrum was Wilt's home court. Daily News archives

Sixers Records: 1967-1996

■ Championship season   **Complete Season**   ■■■ **At the Spectrum** ■■■■

	Regular Season		Playoffs		Regular Season		Playoffs	
Season	**W**	**L**	**W**	**L**	**W**	**L**	**W**	**L**
1967—68	62	20	7	6	23	6	1	3
1968—69	55	27	1	4	26	8	0	3
1969—70	42	40	1	4	22	16	0	2
1970—71	47	35	3	4	24	15	1	2
1971—72	30	52	—	—	14	23	—	—
1972—73	9	73	—	—	5	26	—	—
1973—74	25	57	—	—	14	23	—	—
1974—75	34	48	—	—	20	21	—	—
1975—76	46	36	1	2	34	7	0	2
1976—77	50	32	10	9	32	9	7	3
1977—78	55	27	6	4	37	4	4	1
1978—79	47	35	5	4	31	10	3	1
1979—80	59	23	12	6	36	5	7	2
1980—81	62	20	9	7	37	4	6	2
1981—82	58	24	12	9	32	9	7	3
1982—83	**65**	**17**	**12**	**1**	**35**	**6**	**7**	**0**
1983—84	52	30	2	3	32	9	0	3
1984—85	58	24	8	5	34	7	5	1
1985—86	54	28	6	6	31	10	4	2
1986—87	45	37	2	3	28	13	1	1
1987—88	36	46	—	—	27	14	—	—
1988—89	46	36	0	3	30	11	0	1
1989—90	53	29	4	6	34	7	4	1
1990—91	44	38	4	4	29	12	2	1
1991—92	35	47	—	—	23	18	—	—
1992—93	26	56	—	—	15	26	—	—
1993—94	25	57	—	—	15	26	—	—
1994—95	24	58	—	—	14	27	—	—
1995—96	18	64	—	—	11	30	—	—
Totals	**1,262**	**1,116**	**105**	**90**	**745**	**402**	**59**	**34**

"It was an electrifying moment," Williams says. "It was so fast, people didn't realize what had happened."

It was where the Sixers' Darryl Dawkins shattered a backboard with a dunk and was summoned to the league office in New York to be rebuked by commissioner Larry O'Brien. It was where rookie Mike Dunleavy was told before the '76-77 opener that he had a phantom strained hamstring and was being placed on the injured list to clear roster space for Erving.

It was where the '82-83 Sixers won the first two games of the Finals, then took the next two in LA, excising the memories of Sixers losses to the Trail Blazers in '76-77 and the Lakers in '79-80 and '81-82.

Wilt works against archrival Bill Russell.
Daily News archives

Hal Greer
shoots between
Cincinnati Royals
stars Jerry Lucas
and Oscar
Robertson in
January 1968.
ELWOOD P. SMITH /
Daily News

The Spectrum was, at times, also an NBA showcase for the opponents, including Game 6 of the '79-80 Finals. That was when 6-9 rookie point guard Magic Johnson, jumping center in the absence of the ailing Kareem Abdul-Jabbar, spectacularly put together 42 points, 15 rebounds, seven assists and three steals to lead the Lakers to a 123-107 victory and the championship.

It was also home to the theater of the bizarre as Williams brought in all sorts of acts to pump up the entertainment value, among them Victor the Wrestling Bear, who took on Eagles special-teams captain Vince Papale in a memorable — and really brief — bout; Dick Allen and the Ebonistics, a doo-wop group fronted by the Phillies slugger, and a Don Nelson Coat Throwing Contest, honoring — we think — the then-Milwaukee Bucks coach who had tossed his green jacket on the court in protest of what he viewed as a bad call by the officials.

There was Luke Jackson, the rugged power forward of the '66-67 champion Sixers, tearing an Achilles' tendon in front of the team bench in December 1968, and Billy Cunningham screaming in agony as he tore up a knee in virtually the same spot in December 1975.

And there was a different kind of pain when the decision was made to tear down the Spectrum.

"There's always pain when the past is removed," Williams says. "There's an emptiness. Normally, the old building is torn down as the new one goes up, so this is not your typical farewell. The Spectrum is an antique. But that's the price of progress." ⑤

Doctor J, Bobby Jones and Charles Barkley in background.
JOHN PAUL FILO / Inquirer

Retired Numbers

15 HAL GREER
Philadelphia 76ers

- 6-2 guard was 10-time All-Star (first 3 with Syracuse Nationals)
- Holds Sixers record with 21,586 points
- Member of '67 NBA champs
- Naismith Hall of Fame ('82)

32 BILLY CUNNINGHAM
Philadelphia 76ers

- 6-6 forward was 4-time All-Star
- 13,626 points
- 6,638 rebounds
- Only Sixer to win NBA title as player ('67) and coach ('83)
- Naismith Hall of Fame ('86)

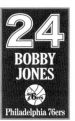

24 BOBBY JONES
Philadelphia 76ers

- 6-9 forward was 4-time All-Star
- 8-time All-Defensive Team
- Sixth Man Award ('83)
- 1983 Phila. Most Courageous Athlete overcame asthma, seizures, heart disorder

6 JULIUS ERVING
Philadelphia 76ers

- 6-7 dunking pioneer was 11-time NBA All-Star after being 3-time ABA MVP
- 1981 NBA MVP
- 18,364 points as Sixer, 30,026 as a pro
- Naismith Hall of Fame ('93)

13 WILT CHAMBERLAIN
Philadelphia 76ers

- 7-2 center was 13-time All-Star, 4-time MVP
- 31,419 points
- 23,924 rebounds
- Only NBA player with a 100-point game
- Naismith Hall of Fame ('79)

10 MAURICE CHEEKS
Philadelphia 76ers

- 6-1 point guard was 4-time All-Star
- Retired in '93 as NBA's all-time steals leader (2,130), fifth in assists (7,392)
- 12,195 total points
- Head coach (2005-08)

34 CHARLES BARKLEY
Philadelphia 76ers

- 6-5 forward was 11-time All-Star (9 with Sixers)
- 23,757 points
- 12,546 rebounds
- Two-time Olympic gold medalist
- Naismith Hall of Fame ('06)

GERARD C. BENENE / Inquirer

At far left, Sixers star
Billy Cunningham
drives past Kareem
Abdul-Jabbar (then
known as Lew Alcindor)
en route to setting the
team's playoff scoring
record of 50 points
on April 1, 1970. Above,
'The Kangaroo Kid'
suffers a knee injury
in December 1975.
He eventually switched
to coaching, leading
the team to the world
championship
in 1983 (left).

MICHAEL MERCANTI / Daily News

Coach Jack Ramsay (left) and Wali Jones (right) on a somber bench in 1970-71. ELWOOD P. SMITH / Daily News

'Dancing Harry' is pretty fly for a white guy. J. KINGSTON COLEMAN / Inquirer

Eagles' Vince Papale doesn't look invincible against Victor the Wrestling Bear at halftime of a 1981 game. ELWOOD P. SMITH / Daily News

Darryl Dawkins goes up for a shot in 1977 with teammate Doug Collins and coach Gene Shue watching.

ELWOOD P. SMITH / Daily News

Maurice Cheeks takes it to the hole in 1987. GEORGE REYNOLDS / Daily News

Dennis Wyndar, 18, has just scored a ticket for Game 1 of the 1983 Finals against the Lakers. MICHAEL VIOLA / Daily News

Julius Erving winds up for his 'Rock the baby to sleep' dunk over Michael Cooper in January 1983.
MICHAEL MERCANTI / Daily News

Nobody wants any part of Moses Malone on this dunk during Game 1 of the 1983 Finals.

GEORGE REYNOLDS / Daily News

Sixers PA announcer Dave Zinkoff shakes the large hand of Wilt Chamberlain in December 1980. BRAD BOWER / Daily News

Willie Burton on the night he broke the Spectrum record with 53 points against the Miami Heat. GEORGE REYNOLDS / Daily News

Manute Bol, the 7-7 Washington center who later became a Sixer, poses with 6-10 Carl Nelson, saluted as the tallest fan to attend the game in December 1985.
GEORGE REYNOLDS / Daily News

Sixers alumni on hand for Spectrum farewell in 1996: from left, Bobby Jones, Maurice Cheeks, Julius Erving, Pat Williams, Al Domenico and Clint Richardson. YONG KIM / Daily News

The changeover crew gets in a little pickup ball at 6 a.m. after setting up the court.
ROGER BARONE

Jerry Stackhouse helps slam the door shut on the Sixers' era at the Spectrum before they moved across the parking lot in 1996.

YONG KIM / Daily News

The Sixers returned to the Spectrum one last time March 13, 2009, and so did some of their all-time greats. Above, Ed Snider greets Julius Erving. Below, Andre Iguodala (right) and Thaddeus Young celebrate their 104-101 win over the Bulls.

Scott May, Most Outstanding Player of the 1976 Final Four, holds the championship hardware, flanked by coach Bobby Knight and Quinn Buckner.

ELWOOD P. SMITH / Daily News

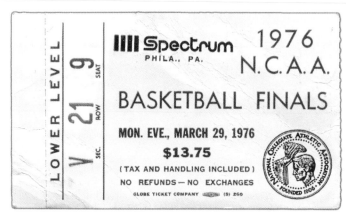

■■■■ CHAPTER FOUR ■■■■

College
Hoops

Big East and A-10 classics,
Bobby Knight's two national titles,
and one of the greatest games ever.

By Dick Jerardi

THERE WAS THE PERFECT TEAM in 1976, the perfect game in 1992, two NCAA championships won, a shot nobody will forget, nearly five-dozen Villanova games — including a blowout of North Carolina, Big East classics with Georgetown, Connecticut, St. John's and Syracuse, close losses to fellow Final Four teams St. John's and Georgetown in 1985 that portended the win over the Hoyas for that year's national championship, and an upset of No. 3 Pittsburgh in the final college game in the building — and Atlantic 10 championships won by Temple (twice) and Saint Joseph's.

That was the Spectrum and college basketball. There was also an East Regional championship in 1980, Iowa winning by a single point over Georgetown, with two eventual Hall of Fame coaches on the sideline, Lute Olson (Iowa) and John Thompson (Georgetown). La Salle used the Spectrum as its home court for two seasons in the mid-1990s. And that regrettable Big 5 half-round-robin found a home there for half of its 8-year run in the 1990s.

Bobby Knight talks to the troops during semifinal win over UCLA in 1976.
Inquirer archives

Glen Grunwald is a gripping figure after the Hoosiers win the national championship in 1981. SUSAN WINTERS / Daily News

College basketball's last perfect team finished its 32-0 season at the Spectrum on March 29, 1976. Five years later, the same school came back to the Spectrum with different players and won another national championship. The same coach was there for both. Bob Knight has not forgotten a single detail from those Final Fours.

The legendary coach has the chairs he sat in during those two championship games in his home. When he was still coaching, he used to sit in one of them for inspiration after losses.

"I sat in one to remind me that we did win one," Knight was saying in a 2009 interview.

Knight's 1976 Indiana team was perfect coming to Philadelphia. It was the second year two teams from the same conference could be in the tournament. The Big Ten was so strong that season that Indiana played Michigan for the title.

After Bobby Wilkerson was knocked out cold in the

first 2 minutes, Indiana trailed at the half, 35-29.

"We were just kind of confused from then on for the rest of the half," Knight says. "I don't think we could have played any better than we did in that second half."

How good was Indiana in those final 20 minutes? The Hoosiers outscored Michigan, 57-33, in the second half and ended their perfect season in style, 86-68.

In 1981, the Indiana team was staying in the now-defunct Cherry Hill Inn, across Route 38 from the Cherry Hill Mall. So were a bunch of fans from LSU, the team Indiana was to play in the semifinals. And those fans kept chanting "Tiger bait, Tiger bait" whenever they saw anyone from Indiana.

"I said, 'So what, just get those kids together and tell them in no way to respond,'" Knight remembers telling his staff.

After Indiana beat LSU, Knight was walking in

'The City of Hoosierly Love'

The NCAA Men's Basketball Final Four was held at the Spectrum twice, and each time it was won by Bobby Knight's Indiana Hoosiers. Here's a breakdown of IU's two championship runs:

1976: The Perfect Season

The 1976 Indiana Hoosiers were the last team to win the finals with a perfect record.

Game	Opponent	Score
Mideast quarterfinal	St. John's	90-70
Mideast semifinal	Alabama	74-69
Mideast final	Marquette	65-56
National semifinal	UCLA	65-51
Final	Michigan	86-68

1981: Isiah's Year

Sophomore Isiah Thomas led the team to its fourth title and won the award for Most Outstanding Player. Later that year, he was drafted by the Detroit Pistons.

Game	Opponent	Score
Mideast quarterfinal	Maryland	99-64
Mideast semifinal	UAB	87-72
Mideast final	St. Joseph's	78-46
National semifinal	LSU	67-49
Final	N. Carolina	63-50

the hotel with one of the vice presidents at Indiana. They had to go through the bar area to the restaurant where they were going to eat.

Knight says he could not resist when, "Some guy said, 'Well, coach, you beat us today.' I said, 'We weren't Tiger bait after all, were we?' And the guy starts going, 'Knight's an a------, Knight's an a------.' "

Knight went back and, according to the coach, "The guy actually slipped, hit the wall and just went down like a raw egg sliding down a wall. He knocked over a trash barrel on himself. That's how it came to be that I threw him in the trash can."

Isiah Thomas takes aim in the Hoosiers' 1981 semifinal win over LSU. NORMAN Y LONO / Daily News

Knight also allows as how he might have "grabbed the guy by the arm" and kind of "spun and pushed him away."

Two mornings later, President Reagan was shot in Washington. The championship game that night with North Carolina was in peril. Only Knight did not know it.

"I did not know Reagan had been shot until I was walking down the ramp into the Spectrum," says Knight. "I'd slept all afternoon. I'm just kind of walking along. I can still see a whole slew of writers coming out of the building, asking, 'Coach, do you think the game should be played?' I said, 'Why the hell wouldn't we play?' I was kind of dumbfounded."

He got clued in quickly. Knight, North Carolina coach Dean Smith and the presidents of the two schools huddled. The presidents asked the coaches what they thought.

"I said, 'We as a country go on,' " Knight remembers saying to the presidents whom he credited with being most responsible for playing the game. So, they played it.

Indiana, behind a brilliant performance from Isiah Thomas, won, 63-50. The Hoosiers had held LSU to 49 in the semis.

"Defense was the hallmark of that team," Knight says, specifically pointing out how critical Landon Turner had been down the stretch against a UNC team that had James Worthy and Sam Perkins on the front line, saying that Turner, not Thomas, was "the best player in the tournament."

Trying to top two national championships should be impossible. It would have been were it not for Duke 104, Kentucky 103 in the NCAA East Regional final on March 28, 1992, and the Christian Laettner shot that won it at the buzzer. To this day, it is the most famous shot in college basketball history.

Christian Laettner launches the most famous shot in college basketball history. CHARLES REX ARBOGAST / AP

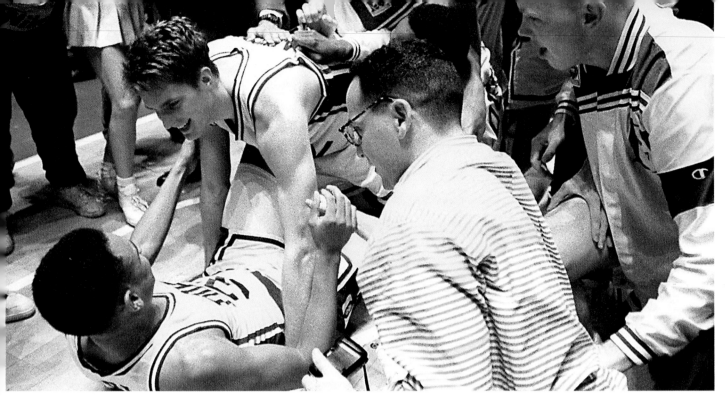

Laettner celebrates with Grant Hill, whose long inbounds pass made the winning shot possible. AMY SANCETTA / AP

The Greatest Game

Widely considered the best game in NCAA Tournament history, the 1992 East Regional final at the Spectrum was highlighted by Christian Laettner's perfect shooting.

	1st	2nd	OT	Total
Duke	50	43	11	104
Kentucky	45	48	10	103

Duke Blue Devils

Player	FG	FGA	FG%	3PT	3PTA	3PT%	FT	FTA	FT%	RB	A	PTS
Christian Laettner	10	10	100.0	1	1	100.0	10	10	100.0	7	3	31
Bobby Hurley	6	12	50.0	5	10	50.0	5	6	83.3	3	10	22
Thomas Hill	6	10	60.0	2	3	66.7	5	5	100.0	3	2	19
Brian Davis	3	6	50.0	0	2	0.0	7	10	70.0	5	1	13
Grant Hill	5	10	50.0	0	0	—	1	2	50.0	10	7	11
Antonio Lang	2	2	100.0	0	0	—	0	1	0.0	3	0	4
Cherokee Parks	2	2	100.0	0	0	—	0	0	—	0	0	4
Marty Clark	0	0	—	0	0	—	0	0	—	0	0	0
Totals	**34**	**52**	**65.4**	**8**	**16**	**50.0**	**28**	**34**	**82.4**	**31**	**23**	**104**

Kentucky Wildcats

Player	FG	FGA	FG%	3PT	3PTA	3PT%	FT	FTA	FT%	RB	A	PTS
Jamal Mashburn	11	16	68.8	3	4	75.0	3	3	100.0	10	3	28
Sean Woods	9	15	60.0	1	1	100.0	2	2	100.0	2	9	21
Dale Brown	6	11	54.5	3	5	60.0	3	5	60.0	3	0	18
John Pelphrey	5	7	71.4	3	4	75.0	3	3	100.0	1	5	16
Richie Farmer	2	3	66.7	1	2	50.0	4	6	66.7	1	1	9
Gimel Martinez	2	4	50.0	1	2	50.0	0	0	—	0	1	5
Deron Feldhaus	2	6	33.3	0	2	0.0	1	2	50.0	1	5	5
Aminu Timberlake	0	0	—	0	0	—	1	2	50.0	0	0	1
Travis Ford	0	2	0.0	0	1	0.0	1	2	50.0	1	0	0
Andre Riddick	0	0	—	0	0	—	0	0	—	0	0	0
Nehemiah Braddy	0	1	0.0	0	0	—	0	0	—	0	0	0
Totals	**37**	**65**	**56.9**	**12**	**21**	**57.1**	**18**	**25**	**72.0**	**21**	**24**	**103**

Temple coach John Chaney works some of his postseason magic, coaxing a 13-14 Owls team to an upset of 22-6 Rutgers in the 1983 Atlantic 10 semifinals. DENIS O'KEEFE / Daily News

Sean Woods made that impossible runner off glass and the overtime clock stopped at 2.1 seconds, with Kentucky leading, 103-102, as Duke took its last timeout.

With the Final Four and defense of Duke's 1991 national title on the line, Laettner set up at the opposite foul line as Grant Hill took the ball from referee Tim Higgins on the baseline. The pass was true. Laettner jumped to catch the ball. He turned to his right, took a dribble with his left hand, turned back to his left and faded away from the rim. He was about 17 feet from the basket when he took the shot with 0.4 on the clock. The buzzer went off when the ball was halfway to the rim.

It was the 10th shot Laettner had taken from the field that night. He had taken 10 shots from the foul line. He had not missed. And he did not miss that final shot.

"There was some doubt," Laettner was saying a few years later. "I felt like it came off pretty nice, but you've just got to watch it for another split-second and all the doubt is taken away. When I let it go, I felt like it had a good chance. But I wasn't sure."

He should have been. That game, he was never going to miss.

Duke's Hall of Fame coach Mike Krzyzewski, a player for Knight at Army, said: "I think the fact that Philadelphia has such an amazing basketball tradition and, although it wasn't one of the Philadelphia teams, it was so good that that game was played in a basketball city, in a city that not just likes basketball, but loves basketball, that has a soul for basketball."

How good was the game? Duke shot 65.4 percent, Kentucky 56.9 percent. The teams were 71-for-117 from the field, 20-for-36 from the arc and 46-for-59 from the line. They scored 207 points in 45 minutes. Basketball could not be played much better, especially with the stakes so high.

Given that there were approximately 200 college basketball games at the Spectrum through the years, the odds on having so many memorable games are quite small. But the memories of those games, those players, those coaches, those teams will live on long after the building itself disappears. S

Lynn Greer jumps into a teammate's arms after hitting three free throws to help nail down an A-10 Tournament win over George Washington in 2001.

YONG KIM / Daily News

Owls Nation is fired up during 1987 Atlantic 10 final victory over West Virginia. BOB LARAMIE / Daily News

Immaculata College's Lori Gable (right) chases a loose ball in the Mighty Macs' Spectrum game against Old Dominion on Jan. 21, 1978.

DENNIS DAYLOR

Rashid Bey was named Most Outstanding Player when the Hawks beat Rhode Island for the 1997 A-10 title.
JERRY LODRIGUSS / Inquirer

Penn's Paul Chambers drives against La Salle's
Randy Woods in January 1992. GEORGE REYNOLDS / Daily News

Allen Iverson didn't play at the Spectrum as a Sixer,
but he did with Georgetown. ALEJANDRO A. ALVAREZ / Daily News

The Quaker City
Jazz Festival opens
the Spectrum on
Sept. 30, 1967.
Spectrum archives

The Grateful Dead

performed a record 53 times in the Spectrum from 1968 to 1995. Here are the dates of each show:

Dec. 6, 1968
Sept. 21, 1972
March 24, 1973
Sept. 20, 1973
Sept. 21, 1973
April 22, 1977
May 13, 1978
Jan. 5, 1979
Jan. 12, 1979
Nov. 5, 1979
Nov. 6, 1979
Aug. 29, 1980
Aug. 30, 1980
May 2, 1981
May 4, 1981
April 5, 1982
April 6, 1982
April 25, 1983
April 26, 1983
April 6, 1985
April 7, 1985
April 8, 1985
March 23, 1986
March 24, 1986
March 25, 1986
March 29, 1987
March 30, 1987
March 31, 1987
Sept. 22, 1987
Sept. 23, 1987
Sept. 24, 1987
Sept. 8, 1988
Sept. 9, 1988
Sept. 11, 1988
Sept. 12, 1988
Oct. 18, 1989
Oct. 19, 1989
Oct. 20, 1989
Sept. 10, 1990
Sept. 11, 1990
Sept. 12, 1990
March 16, 1992
March 17, 1992
March 18, 1992
Sept. 12, 1993
Sept. 13, 1993
Sept. 14, 1993
Oct. 5, 1994
Oct. 6, 1994
Oct. 7, 1994
March 17, 1995
March 18, 1995
March 19, 1995

NOT GOOD FOR ADMISSION

The
Music

'The House That Rock Built' gave us moments that still resound in our hearts and minds (and eardrums).

By Jonathan Takiff

W HEN OUT-OF-TOWNERS TALK of Philadelphia's love affair with its teams, they usually name-check the Flyers or Phillies, Sixers or Eagles.

But I'd argue that our city has been equally supportive of its adopted musical teams — scrappy, street fighting men like the Rolling Stones, Billy Joel, Bruce Springsteen & the E Street Band, the Grateful Dead, Metallica, Public Enemy and The Who.

While these players might have hailed from London, Long Island or San Francisco, Philadelphia played a crucial role in establishing them as major attractions on a national and world scale. And much of the credit for that goes to the Spectrum, one of the first large arenas in the country to recognize

Cat Stevens played the Spectrum in 1974 and '76.
ROGER BARONE

that something new and important was happening in popular culture from the late-'60s forward — a shift in public interest to ambitious, album-oriented music that reflected what the members of the emerging boomer generation were thinking about; music they'd embrace as part of their essential code. Oh, and would willingly camp out in a ticket line overnight to be able to see.

"Other [arena] buildings were afraid of bringing in contemporary music," recalls Electric Factory Concerts/Live Nation impresario Larry Magid. "They used to send around something called a yellow sheet that warned about this act or that — like Alice Cooper with his guillotine, or Black Sabbath's Ozzy Osbourne, supposedly biting off the head of a bat." (A "gross exaggeration," the Oz Man told us.) "But Ed Snider and the Spectrum kept an open mind. This place took risks, actively supported the concert business and in many ways allowed us to innovate."

Stephen Stills, David Crosby and Graham Nash visited three times as Crosby, Stills and Nash. ROGER BARONE

The Spectrum literally opened its doors with music — with Norristown native Jimmy Smith — king of Hammond Organ jazz — as the first act at the two-day Quaker City Jazz Festival on Sept. 30, 1967. Magid wasn't yet part of that event's promoting team — club (Showboat Jazz Theatr and Electric Factory) operators Herb, Jerry and Allen Spivak, with whom he'd soon align as chief talent booker. But Magid was there as a spectator (snappy soul jazz was then huge in this town) and remembers the opening night being so down to the wire "they hadn't even put in the seats in some parts of the building. You'd look up at a section and people were just standing there, all through the show" — later to become a regular Spectrum tradition for fans to demonstrate how much they were into the music.

Fueled by progressive rock FM radio stations like

WMMR that allowed individual DJs to play what they liked, rather than off some national playlist picked by a distant program consultant, dozens of acts were "breaking" out of Philadelphia in the late-1960s and '70s. A Springsteen or James Taylor, Elton John or The Who might first play at the Main Point coffeehouse in Bryn Mawr or the original Electric Factory, a converted tire warehouse at 22nd and Arch Streets, but the artists and the scene quickly outgrew the clubs and graduated to the Spectrum. The "First Annual Quaker City Rock Festival" was the premier rock event in the building, held Oct. 9, 1968, and featuring the likes of Big Brother and the Holding Company (with Janis Joplin), the Chambers Brothers, Buddy Guy, Moby Grape and a headlining Vanilla Fudge. The event proved so successful that a "Second Annual" Quaker City Rock Festival was staged all of

Bob Dylan graced the Spectrum stage seven times. ROGER BARONE

ROGER BARONE

Pete Townshend (left) and Roger Daltrey played the Spectrum six times with The Who. Below: One of Keith Moon's drumsticks from the Dec. 4, 1975 show. ROGER BARONE

6 weeks later! "We figured that some of the people from the first show were still there," muses Magid. Or at least, thought they were.

Concerts became such a crucial part of the Spectrum's identity that *Billboard* magazine hailed the venue as "The House That Rock Built." The music-trade publication also cited the building several times in the '70s and '80s as "Concert Venue of the Year" based on its dozens of shows and huge attendance. And the good vibes didn't hurt.

Despite its large capacity — accommodating up to 19,000 if the artist played in the round, as the likes of Yes and Peter Gabriel, Frank Sinatra and Neil Diamond preferred, or 17,000 tops with a more typical end-stage and "dance concert" setup (that's an Electric Factory/ Spectrum euphemism and innova-

tion for no seats on the floor) — the building's compact design and bright acoustics made the acts seem within reach.

The bands also felt the love in their hearts and chests, as the applause and cheers would "flood back" to the stage, say those who've played. Billy Joel, for one, has "great memories of the way the audience there welcomes us. I can still hear the roar of those crowds ringing in my ears."

"It's almost the air in there is different," seconds Phish front man Trey Anastasio, who grew up in the region and started visiting the Spectrum "with my dad in '75 or '76 when I was 12" — to catch Flyers games and experience his first rock concert with Pink Floyd doing one of its multimedia, quad-sound, "Dark Side of the Moon" spectaculars. "That became the blue-

WHO 12-4-75
KEITH MOON - SPECTRUM

ROGER BARONE

Elvis Presley
played his
fifth and final
Spectrum show
May 28, 1977,
less than 3
months before
his death.

ROGER BARONE

Liza Minnelli, Sammy Davis Jr. and Frank Sinatra sang together Sept. 27 and 28, 1988. Spectrum archives

Phish's Trey Anastasio went to Flyers games at the Spectrum as a youth. SCOTT WEINER

print for what an arena concert is ... what the building would look like when you walked in ... where they put the speakers, hung the light show," Anastasio says. "The thing I remember most when we started playing there was the sound. The Spectrum's got a certain echo to it. It was so exciting for me to be inside that, making music in the room where I heard the screaming when Reggie Leach scored his 50th goal, the same sound when Bruce walked on stage."

Most every act worth its salt played the Spectrum — from The King (Elvis Presley) to Queen to Prince — with some, like Joel and the record-holding Grateful Dead, returning so often that the facility would present and hang banners in the rafters to mark the occasion of a 25th or 40th show — just like the Flyers or 76ers would earn when they won at least a division title. "The only major talent who never played here was John Lennon," Magid says. "We were working on doing a show with him, when he died." Because music in the Spectrum age had become intimately aligned with social protest and spiritual awakening, the venue also played host to some unlikely concert attractions — the Rev. Dr. Martin Luther King Jr. spoke as special guest of Harry Belafonte in 1967, the Maharishi Mahesh Yogi with the Beach Boys a year later.

Rod Stewart, always a big draw, totaled 19 Spectrum shows.
ROGER BARONE

Pink Floyd's Roger Waters was inspired to write 'Comfortably Numb' — the classic cut from the band's rock opera 'The Wall' — by his experience with heavy pain medication during this 1977 Spectrum concert. ROGER BARONE

Not that every act got the royal treatment, of course, from Spectrum showgoers. In 1970, the Doors faced an audience so agitated and pushy (maybe from delays) that the fire marshal was threatening to cancel it. (You can hear Magid's warnings to the audience to chill out on the CD, "The Doors: Live in Philadelphia.")

If you were sloppy drunk and acting stupid, as Rod Stewart (with Faces) did his first of 19 times through, you could fall on your face figuratively and literally. Illness also took its toll. Spectators at Pink Floyd's 1977 "Animals" show remember Roger Waters being off his game the second night. In fact, he was in such pain, he'd been shot up with something strong. Then when the medicine wore off, Waters had to be carted off to a hospital, missing the encore. Something good came from it, though — his classic "Comfortably Numb."

Some openers on a two- or three-act bill were talked over or otherwise snubbed — either because the kids in the band hadn't gotten their stage thing together (poor Steely Dan) or the headliner's audience didn't have a clue who these guys were, a problem even Bruce

A Grateful Dead fan looks for a 'miracle' ticket.
E.W. FAIRCLOTH / Daily News

Luciano Pavarotti is ready to take the ice after receiving a Flyers jersey from Ed Snider in 1985. AMY SANCETTA / AP

Springsteen & the E Street Band faced as the '73 opening act for their Top 40-friendly label mate Chicago.

But if the planets were aligned, a band could go out there a newcomer and return to its dressing room 50 minutes later as a star. One reviewer wrote of Lynyrd Skynyrd as opening act for The Who on Dec. 4, 1973. The Southern rockers faced a crowd so hostile, "it was like someone had thrown red meat on the stage. But by the end of the set, they'd gotten the crowd on their side and even demanding an encore."

For many of us concertgoers, memories of Spectrum events extend beyond the music — which makes its passing from the scene doubly bittersweet. We grew up there. It was our playground. There are the friends we made in the parking lot before a show, the partying 'til we puked (seriously, it was food poisoning), the "miracle" of scoring a ticket to a sold-out concert.

I proposed to my wife Abbe in the Spectrum press box during a Dire Straits concert (March 2, 1992), echoing a line in their song, "Romeo and Juliet" —

"You and me babe, how about it?" OK, so it took a little while for the message to sink in.

My (previous marriage) daughter Hilary went to her first Grateful Dead show at the Spectrum in utero, and returned to see them at such a tender age she thought they were "puppets" bouncing around on a stage. We mourned together, the day Jerry Garcia and that amazing music died.

But just because this building's coming down doesn't mean we have to forget the thrill of the chase and the joy of discovery — the night we first communed with Crosby, Stills, Nash and Young, Bob Marley and the Wailers or Bob Dylan with The Band. Or the times we got to bask in the reflected glory of a living legend like Ray Charles, Presley or Frank Sinatra (even if he was reading the lyrics off a teleprompter). And how 'bout those nights when the walls seemed to shake and the roof almost blew off from the tumult of an AC/DC, Aerosmith, Led Zeppelin or ZZ Top?

Nah, they can't take that away from us.

The Acts

Close to 1,000 performers have graced the stage at the Spectrum. Here they are, with the number of performances, through May 2009.

{53} Grateful Dead **{32}** Bruce Springsteen **{27}** Yes **{25}** Billy Joel **{22}** Aerosmith **{19}** Jethro Tull • Rod Stewart • Van Halen **{18}** Neil Diamond • Elton John **{17}** Rush **{16}** Beach Boys • Chicago • Country Joe and the Fish • Luther Vandross **{15}** Allman Brothers • Eric Clapton **{13}** AC/DC • Black Sabbath • Genesis **{12}** Bon Jovi • David Bowie • Eagles **{11}** The Kinks • Frank Sinatra • ZZ Top **{10}** Earth, Wind and Fire • J. Geils Band • Moody Blues • Ozzy Osbourne • Tom Petty and the Heartbreakers • Bob Seger and the Silver Bullet Band **{9}** Cinderella • Phil Collins • John Denver • Kiss • Mötley Crüe • Ted Nugent **{8}** Blue Oyster Cult • Cars • The Cure • Def Leppard • Doobie Brothers • Peter Gabriel • Heart • Phish • Santana • Neil Young **{7}** Bad Company • Jeff Beck • Frankie Beverly (and Maze) • Alice Cooper • Deep Purple • Bob Dylan • Fleetwood Mac • Guns N' Roses • Isaac Hayes • Humble Pie • Judas Priest • Lynyrd Skynyrd • Public Enemy • Kenny Rogers • Skid Row • Whispers • Johnny Winter • Stevie Wonder **{6}** James Brown • Chambers Brothers • Ray Charles • Electric Light Orchestra • Emerson, Lake and Palmer • Foghat • Foreigner • Hall and Oates • Iron Maiden • Jefferson Starship • Kansas • Dave Mason • John Cougar Mellencamp • New Edition • Outlaws • Pink Floyd • Queensryche • R.E.M. • Styx • George Thorogood and the Destroyers • The Who • Frank Zappa **{5}** Michael Bolton • Boston • Bobby Brown • Depeche Mode • Ronnie James Dio • Duran Duran • Sheila E. • Eric B. and Rakim • INXS • Jackson Five • Janet Jackson • Journey • Greg Kihn • Gladys Knight • LL Cool J • Loggins and Messina • Madonna • Metallica • O'Jays • Poison • Elvis Presley • Queen • Martha Reeves and the Vandellas • Rolling Stones • Linda Ronstadt • David Lee Roth • Billy Squier • Steely Dan • Teena Marie • Tina Turner • Whitesnake **{4}** Bryan Adams • Bachman Turner Overdrive • Black Crowes • Tommy Conwell • The Dead • DJ Jazzy Jeff and the Fresh Prince • Dokken • Aretha Franklin • Doug E. Fresh • Bill Gaither Trio • Jerry Garcia Band • Granati Brothers • Great White • Sammy Hagar • Hammer • Hooters • Alan Jackson • Led Zeppelin • Mahavishnu Orchestra • Yngwie Malmsteen • Barry Manilow • Hugh Masekela • Buddy Miles • Van Morrison • Youssou N'Dour • Willie Nelson • New Kids on the Block • Stevie Nicks • Parliament Funkadelic • Robert Plant • Prince • Ratt • Lionel Richie • Romantics • Rufus • Run-DMC • Leon Russell • Scorpions • Sly and the Family Stone • Steppenwolf • Keith Sweat • Ten Years After • Tesla • .38 Special • Robin Trower • U2 • Joe Walsh • Whodini • Edgar Winter **{3}** Cannonball Adderley • Alabama • Alice in Chains • Anthrax • Ashford and Simpson • Anita Baker • The Band • Barenaked Ladies • Count Basie • Beastie Boys • Bee Gees • Bell Biv Devoe • Big Daddy Kane • Biscuit • Chuckii Booker • Candlebox • Cheap Trick • Cherelle • Commodores • Crosby, Stills and Nash • The Cult • Charlie Daniels Band • En Vogue • Farrenheit • Rory Gallagher • Marvin Gaye • Amy Grant • Grant Lee Buffalo • Al Green • Guy • Heavy D & the Boys • Honeymoon Suite • Whitney Houston • Ian Hunter • Billy Idol • Iron Butterfly • Isley Brothers • Rick James • Jefferson Airplane • Kid 'N Play • B.B. King • Kool Moe Dee • Levert • Huey Lewis and the News • Lisa Lisa and Cult Jam • Nick Lowe • John Mayall • George Michael • Molly Hatchet • Mountain • Night • Oaktown .357 • Orchestral Manoeuvres in the Dark • Jimmy Page and Robert Plant • Pantera • Henry Paul Band • Luciano Pavarotti • Procol Harum • Psychedelic Furs • Rainbow • REO Speedwagon • Diana Ross • Rossington Collins Band • Savoy Brown • Boz Scaggs • Seals and Crofts • Tommy Shaw • Paul Simon • Sinbad • Slade • Southside Johnny • Jimmy Spheeris • Stetsasonic • Sting • Supertramp • Survivor • Temptations • Three Dog Night • Traffic • Marshall Tucker • Ike Turner • Twisted Sister • UK • Stevie Ray Vaughan • War • Roger Waters • Papa Wemba • Steve Winwood **{2}** Paula Abdul • Herb Alpert and Tijuana Brass • America • Anderson, Bruford, Wakeman and Howe • Angel • Asia • Atlantic Starr • Autograph • Joan Baez • Barooga • Bellamy Brothers • Pat Benatar • Black Oak Arkansas • Blackfoot • Chris Bliss • Blue Steel • Boogie Down Productions • Boyz II Men • Clarence "Gatemouth" Brown • Jackson Browne • Glen Burtnick • Carillo • Johnny Cash • June Carter Cash • Cheetah Girls • Lou Christie • Andrew Dice Clay • Joe Cocker • Natalie Cole • Collective Soul • Bobby Comstock Band • Dane Cook • Billy Ray Cyrus • Dangerous Toys • Dashboard Confessional • Miles Davis • Sammy Davis Jr. • Spencer Davis • The Dells • Rick Derringer • Digital Underground • Donovan • Drivin' and Cryin' • Dr. John • Erasure • Gloria Estefan & the Miami Sound Machine • Deon Estus • Melissa Etheridge • Extreme • Faster Pussycat • Fastway • Fifth Dimension • Firefall • The Firm • Roberta Flack • Flamin' Harry • Dan Fogelberg • 4 Non-Blondes • Four Tops • Peter Frampton • Fuel • Garbage • Georgia Satellites • Johnny Gill • Glass Tiger • Go-Go's • Graham Central Station • Grand Funk Railroad • Jo Jo Gunne • Buddy Guy • George Harrison • Don Henley • Faith Hill • Steve Hillage • Hot Tuna • Freddie Jackson • Jane's Addiction • Joan Jett and the Blackhearts • Jesse Johnson Revue • Tom Jones • Kix • Kool and the Gang • Korn • Krokus • LA Guns • Alvin Lee • Leroux • Ramsey Lewis • Live • Tone Loc • Lone Justice • Loudness • Loverboy • LTD • MC Lyte • Mahogany Rush • Ziggy Marley • Curtis Mayfield • Reba McEntire • Meat Loaf • Megadeth • Menudo • Bette Midler • Midnight Flyer • Frankie Miller • Steve Miller • Milli Vanilli • Liza Minnelli • Eddie Money • Mott the Hoople • Mr. Big • Shirley Murdock • Eddie Murphy • Naughty by Nature • Network • David "Fathead" Newman • Nine Inch Nails • Nitzer Ebb • Oak Ridge Boys • Orleans • Pacific Gas and Electric • Graham Parker • Dolly Parton • Sandi Patti • Charley Pride • Rail • Rascals • Ready for the World • Real Roxanne • Redbone • Red Rider • Mason Ruffner • Rusted Root • SWV • Saga • Mongo Santamaria • Screaming Cheetah Wheelies • Sea Level • Kenny Wayne Shepherd • Smashing Pumpkins • Soup Dragons • Rick Springfield • Squeeze • Starland • Cat Stevens • Stephen Stills • Al B. Sure • Sweet Inspirations • James Taylor • Technotronic • Three Times Dope • Til Tuesday • Trans-Siberian Orchestra • Pat Travers • Triumph • Trixter • Tommy Tutone • UFO • Uriah Heep • UTFO • Vanilla Fudge • Gino Vannelli • Veruca Salt • Rick Wakeman • Wang Chung • Warrant • Dionne Warwick • Waysted • Lawrence Welk • Wet Wet Wet • Y&T • Warren Zevon **{1}** A's • Accept • King Sunny Ade • Adam Ant • Trace Adkins • A Flock of Seagulls • After 7 • After 8 • Air Supply • Aldo Nova • Gregg Allman • Mark Almond • Ambrosia • American Dream • Lee Andrews and the Hearts • Animals • Paul Anka • Susan Anton • Anvil • April Wine • Atari Teenage Riot • Chet Atkins • Average White Band • Babyface • Bad English • Badlands • Balance • Bar-Kays • Billy Barner • Barnstorm • Rob Base • Francesca Beghe • Be Bop Deluxe • Beck, Bogart, Appice • Beck • Harry Belafonte • Bill Bellamy • George Benson • Chuck Berry • Beru Revue • Big Brother and the Holding Company • Big Street • John Bizarre • Biz Markie • Black and Blue • Blasters • Mary J. Blige • Blind Faith • Blondie • Blood, Sweat and Tears • Kurtis Blow • Blow Monkeys • Bobby & the Midnites • Bonnie and Friends • Angela Bofill • Bonham • Booker T & the MGs • Bootsy's Rubber Band • Bourheois Tagg • Boys • Brandy • Breakwater • Brewer and Shipley • Brick • Brides of Funkenstein • Britny Fox • Garth Brooks • Brooks & Dunn • Brothers Johnson • Maxine Brown • Dave Brubeck • Jack Bruce • Jack Bruce and Leslie West • Peabo Bryson • Bullet Boys • Buckinghams • Buckwheat Zydeco • Buffalo Stampede • Bus Boys • Bush • Richard Bush • Red Buttons • Charlie Callas • Cameo • Glen Campbell • Canned Heat • Cardigans • Mariah Carey • Eric Carmen • Paul Carrack • David Cassidy • Shaun Cassidy • Cats • Harry Chapin • Charlie • Checkmates • Cher • Kenny Chesney • Chicken Shack • Chiffons • Petula Clark • Roy Clark • Stanley Clarke • The Clash • Climax Blues Band • The Coasters • Cock Robin • Paula Cole • Commander Cody • Coney Hatch • Ry Cooder • Chick Corea • Elvis Costello • James Cotton Blues Band • Cowboy • Floyd Cramer • Crawler • Cream • Creedence Clearwater Revival • Marshall Crenshaw • Jim Croce • David Crosby • David Crosby and Graham Nash • Norm Crosby • Crosby, Stills, Nash and Young • Andrae Crouch and the Disciples • Cruzados • Culture Club • Burton Cummings • Dakota • Mac Davis • Tyrone Davis • Morris Day • Chris DeBurgh • The Deele • Delaney • De La Soul • Del Fuegos • Del Lords • Del Vikings • Dino • Dion • Dire Straits • Dixianna • Dixie Chicks • The Doors • Dovells • Patti Drew • Drifters • Danny Dooma and Night Eyes • Duprees • Eazy-E • Edison Electric • Electric Guitars • The Emperors • Everest • Exile • Experience Unlimited • Exposé • Fabulous Poodles • The Fabulous Thunderbirds • Faith No More • Fall Out Boy • Family • Fatback • Feelies • Ella Fitzgerald • Five Satins • The Fixx • Bela Fleck and the Flecktones • Flying Burrito Brothers • FM • Ellen Foley • Foo Fighters • Force MD's • 14-Karat Gold • Kirk Franklin and the Family • Ace Frehley • Glenn Frey • Funkadelics • Kenny G • Jeffrey Gaines • Gallagher • Gap Band • Larry Gatlin • Stan Gotz • Ghetto Boys • Debbie Gibson • Astrude Gilbert • Dizzy Gillespie • Girlschool • Giuffria • Richard Glover • Golden Earring • Goldie • Good Charlotte • Good God • Good Rats • Lesley Gore • Larry Graham • Lee Greenwood • H-Town • Merle Haggard • Jimmy Hall • John Hammond • Richie Havens • Edwin Hawkins • Bonnie Hayes • Robert Hazard • Jeff Healey Band • Heaven's Edge • Helix • Jimi Hendrix • John Hiatt • Susanna Hoffs • Groove Holmes • Young Holt • Dr. Hook and the Medicine Show • Horslips • Steve Howe • Hunter and Collectors • Ice Cube • Icehouse • Julio Iglesias • Indigo Girls • Information Society • Iron Horse • Dom Irrera • It Bites • JJ Fadd • Chuck Jackson • Joe Jackson • Jackyl • Jade • James Gang • Tommy James and the Shondells • Jars of Clay • Jayhawks • Waylon Jennings • John Butcher Axis • Michael Johnson • Howard Jones • K's Choice • Chaka Khan • Katrina and the Waves • Alan Kay • Toby Keith • Kid Rock • Carole King • Evelyn "Champagne" King • King Crimson • Kings of Leon • Sam Kinison • Al Kooper • Danny Kortchmar • Dave Koz • Lenny Kravitz • Kwame • Lakeside • Staci Lattisaw • Patti LaBelle • Cyndi Lauper • Julian Lennon • Jay Leno • Level 42 • Jerry Lee Lewis • Life of Agony • Limp Bizkit • David Lindley • Linkin Park • Little Anthony • Little Caesar • Little Feat • Little River Band • Kenny Loggins • Louie Louie • Love and Hate • Love Unlimited • Dr. Martin Luther King Jr. • Jimmy Mack • Manfred Mann • Magnum • Maharishi Mahesh Yogi • Michel'le • Miriam Makeba • Malo • Mama's Pride • Mandrill • Herbie Mann • Marilyn Manson • Bob Marley and the Wailers • Maroon 5 • Esther Marrow • Marseille • John Martyn • Matchbox 20 • Dave Matthews Band • Martina McBride • Paul McCartney and Wings • Michael McDonald • Delbert McClinton • Tim McGraw • Men at Work • Metal Church • Midnight Oil • Midnight Star • Alannah Miles • Stephanie Mills • Miracles • Mission UK • Joni Mitchell • Moby Grape • Models • John Michael Montgomery • Montrose • Paul Mooney • Melba Moore • Morcheeba • Melissa Morgan • Alanis Morissette • Motels • Motörhead • Murphy's Law • Nantucket • Narada • Nazareth • Neighbors Complaint • Tracy Nelson and Mother Earth • New Riders of the Purple Sage • Juice Newton • Olivia Newton-John • Night Ranger • Norton Buffalo Stampede • NWA • Oingo Boingo • One-Way • Opus • Orgy • Tony Orlando and Dawn • Shelyan Orphan • Osibisa • Osmond Brothers • Jimmy Page • Panic at the Disco • John Parr • Don Patterson • Pearl Jam • Joe Perry Project • Pixies • P.J. Harvey • Plain White T's • Pockets • Poco • Police • Pointer Sisters • Jean-Luc Ponty • Poor • Iggy Pop • Dave Porter • Post Office • Power Station • Billy Preston • Pretenders • Primal Scream • Prince Charles and the City Beat Band • Private Life • Prong • Arthur Prysock • Gary Puckett • Pursuit of Happiness • Queen Latifah • Quicksilver • Quiet Riot • Quiver • Raconteurs • Radiohead • Rage Against the Machine • Rammstein • Boots Randolph • Raspberries • Lou Rawl • Red Hot Chili Peppers • Lou Reed • Terry Reid • Renaissance • Rene and Angela • Rentals • Restless Heart • Buddy Rich • Righteous Brothers • Riot • Pinkey Roberts • Holly Robinson • Smokey Robinson and the Miracles • Rockats • Rockets • Rockmaster Scott and Dynamic Three • Paul Rodgers • Roger and Roger • Jim Rose Circus Show • Rough Cutt • Dave Rowland • Todd Rundgren • Nipsey Russell • Bobby Rydell • Sad Café • Salt-N-Pepa • Savatage • Sawyer Brown • Saxon • Gil Scott-Heron • Tom Scott • Sea Train • John Sebastian • Seduction • Semisonic • 707 • Shabba Ranks • Shai • Shakin' Street • Duncan Sheik • Shirelles • Lonnie Shorr • Silk • Silverchair • Sister Sledge • Slaughter • Slayer • Slick Rick • Frankie Smith • Jimmy Smith • Kevin Smith • Michael W. Smith • Smooth Silk • Snoop Dogg • Phoebe Snow • Soul Asylum • Soul Brothers Six • Sparks • Special Beat • Split Enz • Judson Spence • Spinners • Spirit • Stabbing Westward • Michael Stanley Band • Staple Singers • Starr • Starpoint • Sterling • Larry Stewart • Sonny Stitt • Randy Stonehill • Stompers • Stone Temple Pilots • Storm • Stylistics Sugar • Sugar Hill Gang • Suicidal Tendencies • Henry Lee Summer • Sutherland Brothers • Sweet Stavin Chain • Sylvia • System of a Down • T. Rex • Tag Team • 10,000 Maniacs • Testament Theory • The The • BJ Thomas • Thompson Twins • Thrasher Brothers • Three Crosses • 3-D • TKO • TLC • Today • Tony Toni Tone • Oscar Toney Jr. • Tool • Too Short • Tower of Power • Simon Townsend • Tragically Hip • Troop • Joe Lynn Turner • UB40 • Utopia • Johnny Van Zandt • Sarah Vaughn • Velvet Elvis • Velvet Revolver • Virginia Wolf • Michael Walden • Wallflowers • Was (Not Was) • Wasp • Muddy Waters • Weather Girls • Max Webster • Bob Weir and Rob Wasserman • Leslie West • Barry White • Karen White • Wilco • Denise Williams • Flip Wilson • Jackie Wilson • Nancy Wilson • Winger • Neil Young and Stephen Stills • Young M.C. • Zebra

PROMOTER/FACILITY

ROLLING STONES
PHILADELPHIA
JUNE 30

name   authorization

If Keith Richards is trying to be incognito,
it doesn't work. ROGER BARONE

Robert Plant on stage, and (top of next page) in a Spectrum hallway with his Led Zeppelin mates and others.

ROGER BARONE

Did you ever think you'd see a guy named Alice in a Flyers jersey? SCOTT WEINER

Carlos Santana put on eight concerts at the Spectrum. ROGER BARONE

Dolly Parton played in 1985 and 2004.

ZOHRAB KAZANJIAN

Willie 'The Phillie' Nelson visited in 1982, '83, '84 and '85. ZOHRAB KAZANJIAN

June Carter Cash and Johnny Cash. The Man in Black played the Spectrum in 1970 and '71.

ZOHRAB KAZANJIAN

Neil Young (right, behind
Stephen Stills) left Crosby,
Stills, Nash and Young shortly
after this June 29, 1976 visit.

ROGER BARONE

Jethro Tull's Ian Anderson, best known for his scorching flute solos in classic rock anthems like 'Locomotive Breath,' shreds on his violin during one of the band's 19 Spectrum shows. SCOTT WEINER

Rick James' sunglasses probably didn't stay off for long.

MICHAEL MERCANTI / Daily News.

George Harrison performed twice at the Spectrum.
MIKE LESSNER

Billy Joel during
one of his 25
Spectrum shows.
ZOHRAB KAZANJIAN

The Supreme being herself, Diana Ross. ZOHRAB KAZANJIAN

Smokey Robinson is the life of the party.
ZOHRAB KAZANJIAN

Eric Clapton, who first played the Spectrum in 1968 with Cream. SCOTT WEINER

Never guess which band this is. Chicago played the Spectrum 16 times. ZOHRAB KAZANJIAN

On Nov. 22, 1984, Prince parties like it's 1999.
GEORGE REYNOLDS / Daily News

Aerosmith's Steven Tyler, shown in 1994, vowed never to return to the Spectrum after being hit by a glass bottle Nov. 25, 1978. He broke that vow 16 times. Spectrum archives

Romantic crooner Luther Vandross always drew a big crowd. E.W. FAIRCLOTH / Daily News

BORDERS

BORDERS
BOOKS AND MUSIC
1 SOUTH BROAD STREET
PHILADELPHIA PA 19107
(215) 568-7400

STORE: 0021   REG: 04/78 TRAN#: 3776
SALE   12/15/2009 EMP: 00070
                            EMP: 00000

GIFT RECEIPT

GOD BLESS SPECTRUM
9879724   CL T   CKGJ

PA 8%   TAX

12/15/2009 12:53PM

For returns within 60 days of
purchase accompanied by a Borders
Gift Receipt the purchase price
(after applicable discounts) will be
refunded via a gift card.

ted only if presented in saleable condition accom-
d by the original sales receipt or Borders gift receipt
the time periods specified below. Returns accom-
d by the original sales receipt must be made within
ys of purchase and the purchase price will be
led in the same form as the original purchase.
s accompanied by the original Borders gift receipt
be made within 60 days of purchase and the
ase price will be refunded in the form of a return gift

nges of opened audio books, music, videos, video
, software and electronics will be permitted subject
same time periods and receipt requirements as
and can be made for the same item only.
icals, newspapers, comic books, food and drink,
downloads, gift cards, return gift cards, items
d "non-returnable," "final sale" or the like and
-print, collectible or pre-owned items cannot be
ed or exchanged.
s and exchanges to a Borders, Borders Express or
nbooks retail store of merchandise purchased from
s.com may be permitted in certain circumstances.
rders.com for details.

BORDERS.

rns

s of merchandise purchased from a Borders,
s Express or Waldenbooks retail store will be
ted only if presented in saleable condition accom-
by the original sales receipt or Borders gift receipt
the time periods specified below. Returns accom-
by the original sales receipt must be made within
vs of purchase and the purchase price will be
ed in the same form as the original purchase.
s accompanied by the original Borders gift receipt
be made within 60 days of purchase and the
se price will be refunded in the form of a return gift

ges of opened audio books, music, videos, video
, software and electronics will be permitted subject
same time periods and receipt requirements as

Bruce Springsteen and the E Street Band on Dec. 9, 1980, the night after John Lennon was killed. The closing number that night was a tribute to Lennon, 'Twist and Shout.'
ZOHRAB KAZANJIAN

Elton John doesn't skimp on costumes. JOY BANTIVOGITO

The Spectrum became a House of Wonder's when Stevie took the stage. ZOHRAB KAZANJIAN

David Bowie, who found much of his early fan base in Philly, played the Spectrum 12 times. ROGER BARONE

Neil Diamond performs Feb. 6, 1989. BOB LARAMIE / Daily News

Whitney Houston grins during her show Aug. 14, 1987.
ZOHRAB KAZANJIAN

Paul Simon puts on a show in June 1987.
GEORGE REYNOLDS / Daily News

Michael Jackson performs with his brothers.
ZOHRAB KAZANJIAN

Philly's own Boyz II Men.
Spectrum archives

Tina Turner performs with Lionel Richie in May 1984.
ZOHRAB KAZANJIAN

Geddy Lee and Rush played the Spectrum 17 times. Spectrum archives

ZZ Top's Dusty Hill and Billy Gibbons. RICH FUSCIA

David Lee Roth fronts Van Halen in March 1984 in one of the band's 19 Spectrum shows. NORMAN Y. LONO / Daily News

The Eagles perform one of their 12 Spectrum shows, this one during the 1994 'Hell Freezes Over' tour. Spectrum archives

The Red Hot Chili Peppers' Flea and Dave Navarro in February 1996.

Spectrum archives

Michael Stipe during
one of R.E.M.'s six visits.
Spectrum archives

Jon Bon Jovi performed
12 times from 1984 to '93.
BOB LARAMIE / Daily News

Those '70s Shows

The Spectrum's reign as one of the world's leading live-music venues spanned parts of four decades. But there is no question the arena reached its zenith in the 1970s. Here are some of the Spectrum shows that, generations later, still resonate with me.

By Chuck Darrow

Mountain, Black Sabbath and Humble Pie (April 1971)

You always remember your first time; this was my inaugural musical Spectrum visit. Opener Humble Pie (with gritty-voiced Steve Marriott and cutie-pie guitarist Peter Frampton) set the tone with some rough-and-tumble British blues-rock; Black Sabbath, touring behind its epochal "Paranoid" album, shook the rafters with its proto-metal; Mountain was loud and boring thanks to what I recall as guitarist Leslie West's endless (and pointless) soloing.

Black Sabbath, Humble Pie and Alice Cooper (July 1971)

Back then the rule seemed to be that rock musicians must wear jeans and T-shirts and just sort of stand there looking cool. But then along came the opening act, a guy with a girl's name who wore fright makeup, dressed in tattered tights and did things like decapitate a baby doll and sit in a remarkably authentic-looking electric chair. Who knew rock could be so visually over-the-top and entertaining?

Jethro Tull (May 1972)

This was a time when a musically challenging, lyrically obtuse album consisting of a single "song" broken up into two parts (one for each side of the record) could hit the top spot on the Billboard magazine album chart. Which is exactly what Tull's "Thick as a Brick" did. The "Thick" tour was wildly theatrical and not a little goofy (bandleader Ian Anderson mined the same vein of zany British sense of humor as Monty Python). And the show made me a lifelong Tull Head who has seen them about 65 times and counting to date.

The Rolling Stones and Stevie Wonder (July 1972)

This was the first concert tour chronicled by the nation's mainstream media (thus it can be argued it ushered in the modern rock-concert era). My first Stones concert was highlighted by an indelible version of "Midnight Rambler" and killer takes on several tunes from the "Sticky Fingers" album. It also featured the legendary "(I Can't Get No) Satisfaction"/"Uptight (Everything's Alright)" encore for which Wonder joined the Stones.

ROGER BARONE

Rod Stewart & Faces (July 1972)
Backed by the loosey-goosey Faces (including future Stone Ronnie Wood), the rooster-maned rocker put on a show for the ages as he swaggered and shimmied (usually with drink in hand) through a raucous set of future classics including "Maggie May" and "Stay with Me." This tour was also notable for its pioneering use of closed-circuit video.

Pink Floyd (March 1973)
The band's watershed "Dark Side of the Moon" tour used spacey lighting, bizarre video displays and 360-degree sound to turn the Spectrum into a giant spaceship that hurdled fans through the cosmos without ever leaving the ground. The presentation was so relentlessly psychedelic that the use of hallucinogenic drugs that night would have been redundant.

Yes (February 1974)
The ultimate test of fans' endurance, this show (performed on a stage designed to resemble a landscape located somewhere outside this galaxy) started with performances of all four sides of the band's just-released epic, "Tales From Topographic Oceans," and also included the preceding album, "Close to the Edge," in its entirety. Whew!

Paul McCartney & Wings (May 1976)
"Wings Over America," Sir Paul's first post-Beatles road trip, was designed to introduce him as an entity apart from his former incarnation as "the cute Beatle." If memory serves, only a few Fab Four tunes (including "Yesterday" and "Lady Madonna") made the set list, but it didn't matter as Macca and his crackerjack band turned in a diverse, playful and flawlessly rendered show. A bonus: McCartney used "Live and Let Die" to introduce laser lighting to the rock-concert realm.

Elton John (July 1976)
Elton's "Liberace of Rock" era peaked on this tour with over-the-top costuming and lighting, and a huge (by standards of the day) band. The show's opening sequence, the atmospheric "Funeral For A Friend," which segued into a rip-snorting "Love Lies Bleeding," remains one of the greatest concert kickoffs ever.

Bruce Springsteen (October 1976)
Sure The Boss and his turbo-charged E Street Band could rip it up like nobody's business in small clubs like the old Main Point in Bryn Mawr and medium-sized halls like Upper Darby's Tower Theater. But could his act translate to hockey arenas? He opened for jazz rockers Chicago at the Spectrum in June '73; the result was so disheartening, Bruce swore he'd never caddie for any other act ever again. But this, his first-ever headlining date in a mega-auditorium, was a tour de force that announced to the world what Philly had known for several years: Bruce Springsteen was a superstar's superstar.

Joe Frazier initiates the Spectrum's sports legacy with his second-round TKO of Tony Doyle on Oct. 17, 1967.
ALEXANDER DEANS / Inquirer

Oscar Bonavena looks like a guy who just went 15 rounds with Joe Frazier, which he did in Frazier's 1968 victory at the Spectrum. ELWOOD P. SMITH / Daily News

Did We
Mention?

Boxing, tennis, lacrosse, soccer, the Cookie Monster and monster trucks, and everything in between.

By Ed Barkowitz

T IS SOMEWHAT APPROPRIATE that when the games began at the Spectrum, they began with fists rather than pucks or balls. A large chunk of the arena's legacy is grounded in the exploits of the Broad Street Bullies, so it is noteworthy that it was the best Philadelphia heavyweight ever who got things rolling at Broad and Pattison.

The date was Oct. 17, 1967, a Tuesday, when a five-bout card was held at Ed Snider's brand-new baby. Having been preceded by a concert and an ice show, this was the Spectrum's first sporting event.

...And In This Corner

The Spectrum hosted 99 boxing cards. The main events are listed here, winners first.

1967
10/17	Joe Frazier, Tony Doyle	KO2

1968
8/6	Emile Griffith, Gypsy Joe Harris	W12
10/29	Kitten Hayward, Emile Griffith	W10
11/18	Chuck Leslie, Roger Russell	W10
12/10	Joe Frazier, Oscar Bonavena	W15

1969
11/18	Leotis Martin, Roger Russell	W10

1970
7/20	George Foreman, Roger Russell	KO1
10/6	Sammy Goss, Augie Pantellas	W10
11/17	Ricardo Arredondo, Sammy Goss	KO5

1971
1/18	Ricardo Arredondo, Augie Pantellas	KO10
6/22	Cyclone Hart, Don Fullmer	W10
8/10	Bennie Briscoe, Juarez DeLima	KO2
9/21	Cyclone Hart, Denny Moyer	ND6
11/15	Bennie Briscoe, Rafael Gutierrez	KO2

1972
11/20	Sammy Goss, Jose Luis Lopez	W10

1973
1/15	Sammy Goss, Raul Cruz	KO2
1/29	Bennie Briscoe, Carlos Alberto Salinas	KO5
2/19	Ernie Terrell, Bill Drover	KO1
3/5	Willie Monroe, Don Cobbs	W10
3/26	Bennie Briscoe, Art Hernandez	TKO3
4/16	Sammy Goss, Jorge Ramos	W10
5/14	Alfonso Hayman, Miguel Barreto	D10
6/11	Ron Lyle, Wendell Newton	W10
6/25	Bennie Briscoe, Billy Douglas	TKO8
8/6	Tyrone Everett, Jose Valdez	W10
8/31	Alfonso Hayman, Papo Villa	KO7
9/24	Richie Kates, Don Fullmer	W10
10/8	Boogaloo Watts, Carlos Alberto Salinas	KO8
10/22	Bennie Briscoe, Ruben Arocha	KO3
11/12	Cyclone Hart, Al Quinney	KO2
12/3	Tyrone Everett, Richie Villanueva	KO9

1974
1/14	Kitten Hayward, Lil' Abner	KO4
2/18	Willie Monroe, Cyclone Hart	W10
3/11	Sammy Goss, Clemente Mucino	W10
4/8	Willie Monroe, Kitten Haward	TKO7
4/29	Tyrone Everett, Sammy Goss	W12
5/22	Alfonso Hayman, Roy Barrientos	W10
7/15	Boogaloo Watts, Cyclone Hart	KO1
8/19	Willie Monroe, Billy Douglas	W10
9/10	Tyrone Everett, Jose Luis Madrid	KO2
10/9	Emile Griffith, Bennie Briscoe	W10
11/12	Boogaloo Watts, Willie Monroe	W10

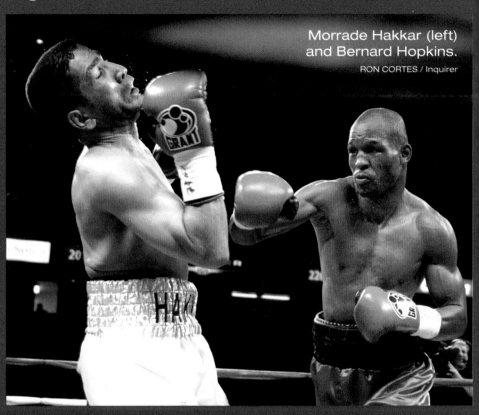

Morrade Hakkar (left) and Bernard Hopkins.
RON CORTES / Inquirer

Marvin Hagler (left) and Willie Monroe. SAM PSORAS / Daily News

1975
1/14	Tyrone Everett, Bert Nabalatan	W10
2/17	Mike Rossman, Matt Donovan	W10
3/11	Tyrone Everett, Jose Luis Lopez	KO4
4/7	Bennie Briscoe, Vinnie Curto	D10
5/5	Tyrone Everett, Pedro Aguero	W10
6/16	Bennie Briscoe, Kitten Hayward	W10
7/24	Tyrone Everett, Hyun Chai Kim	KO6
8/18	Bennie Briscoe, Eddie Gregory	W10
9/16	Tyrone Everett, Benjamin Ortiz	W10
10/21	Duane Bobick, Rochelle Norris	KO2
11/18	Bennie Briscoe, Cyclone Hart	D10

1976
1/13	Boogaloo Watts, Marvin Hagler I	W10
2/10	Tyrone Everett, Rosalio Muro	W12
3/9	Willie Monroe, Marvin Hagler I	W10
4/6	Bennie Briscoe, Cyclone Hart II	KO1
5/19	Willie Monroe, Felton Marshall	TKO7
8/16	David Love, Willie Monroe	KO4
9/14	Marvin Hagler, Cyclone Hart	TKO9
11/30	Alfredo Escalera, Tyrone Everett	W15

1977
1/17	Bennie Briscoe, Karl Vinson	W10
2/21	Tyrone Everett, Memo Vega	KO8
6/27	Jerome Artis, Red Berry	W10
7/26	Matt Franklin, Marvin Johnson I	KO12
8/23	Marvin Hagler, Willie Monroe III	KO2
9/17	Roberto Duran, Edwin Viruet	W15
11/1	Matt Franklin, Lee Royster	W10

1978
1/17	Augie Pantellas, Issac Vega	TKO5
2/10	Matt Franklin, Richie Kates	KO6
3/14	Augie Pantellas, Roman Contreras	W10
4/10	Victor Abraham, Jimmy Rothwell	W10
5/24	Mike Rossman, Lonnie Bennett	KO2
6/19	Matt Franklin, Dale Grant	KO5
8/24	Marvin Hagler, Bennie Briscoe	W10
9/27	Bobby Chacon, Augie Pantellas	KO7
10/24	Matt Franklin, Yaqui Lopez I	TKO11
12/5	Mike Rossman, Aldo Traversaro	TKO6

Alfredo Escalera sinks his teeth
into Tyrone Everett's forehead.

ZOHRAB KAZANJIAN

1979

2/5	David Love, Bennie Briscoe	W10
4/3	Thomas Hearns, Alfonso Hayman	W10
5/14	Curtis Parker, Willie Warren	KO5
7/16	Curtis Parker, Willie Monroe	W10
9/11	Curtis Parker, Elisha Obed	TKO7
11/14	Jerry Martin, Jesse Burnett	W12

1980

| 2/1 | Jeff Chandler, Javier Flores | KO10 |

1981

| 5/18 | Jerry Martin, Leon McDonald | KO7 |

1982

| 8/7 | Dwight Braxton, Saad Muhammad II | TKO6 |

1983

| 9/9 | Jimmie Sykes, Steve Traitz Jr. | KO4 |
| 11/10 | Frank Montgomery, Garland Wright | W8 |

1995

| 12/16 | Mike Tyson, Buster Mathis Jr. | KO3 |

2002

| 5/17 | Luis Alberto Santiago, Mambea Bakari | W10 |
| 10/11 | Chucky T, Ivan Robinson | W10 |

2003

1/24	Michael Grant, Carlton Johnson	TKO5
3/29	Bernard Hopkins, Morrade Hakkar	TKO8
6/20	Demetrius Hopkins, Shakha Moore	TKO1
11/11	Mike Stewart, Ivan Robinson	TKO8

2005

| 3/24 | Robert Hawkins, John Poore | TKO5 |

2006

| 11/9 | Harry Joe Yorgey, Martinus Clay | D10 |

2007

| 10/19 | Richard Stewart, Jameel Wilson | D8 |

SOURCE: www.phillyboxinghistory.com

Bennie Briscoe lands a solid punch on Bob Patterson
on May 24, 1978. ELWOOD P. SMITH / Daily News

The *Daily News* reported that a crowd of 8,404 showed up
and the gross gate of $51,836 would allow the show's promot-
ers to just about break even. Those in attendance got a quick
glimpse of a hometown fighter who would go on to become
one of the greatest in history.

Using a series of body shots in the first round and a couple
of fierce left hooks in the second, Joe Frazier quickly dispensed
of Tony Doyle, a courageous but distracted pug out of Utah.

"He is clever ... a nice boxer," Frazier said afterward. "But
he has been worried about his family. I figured, let's get him
home to see them."

Doyle's wife, Carol, had given birth to twins 8 days before and there were complications. The boys were delivered 6
weeks prematurely.

"My mind wasn't on the fight," recalls Doyle, now a 64-year-
old paint contractor living in Utah. "It was a super big thing
for me because Salt Lake City was a small town and I had
never fought in an environment like that. The crowd was real
tough and Joe was coming up the ranks as a fighter."

Frazier, now also 64, was "coming up the ranks" like a freight
train on the open tracks. The victory at the Spectrum ran his
record to 18-0 and the TKO, at 1 minute, 4 seconds of the second
round, was his 16th knockout. Though the main event lasted less
than 5 minutes, it was a promising start for the new building.

Protesters greet the arrival of the Soviet gymnasts in 1974. Temple University Libraries Urban Archives

Gymnastics

Olga Korbut's triple-gold-medal performance at the 1972 Olympics was overshadowed by the tragedy of murderous kidnappers and the triumph of Mark Spitz. When the Russian gymnast came to the Spectrum for an exhibition in 1974, she was met with fanfare and discord. The Cold War was still frosty and the thought of Russians dancing around in the nation's birthplace was disconcerting to many; so much so that Spectrum officials felt compelled to take out the following advertisement explaining the event:

On Saturday, Nov. 9 at 1 p.m. and Sunday, Nov. 10 at noon, the Spectrum presents the USSR Men's and Women's National Gymnastic team.

We are doing this for a number of reasons.

First, we are anxious to encourage sports and cultural exchange between the two countries.

Second, we are interested in promoting gymnastics.

Third, we are interested in focusing attention upon Philadelphia.

Our presenting the match in no way diminishes our concern for Soviet Jewry who are not permitted the same opportunities as other groups in Russia.

And we hope this people-to-people contact will help in some small way to open the doors of the Soviet Union wide enough to grant freedom to the oppressed people there.

Therein lie some of the reasons so many Americans celebrated the Flyers' victory over the Soviet Red Army in 1976 and even more learned to believe in miracles when Team USA beat the Russians in the 1980 Olympic hockey semifinals.

Phantoms fans and bench erupt at end of Calder Cup-clinching victory in 1998. LEN REDKOLES

Phantoms

When the Flyers vacated the Spectrum for the CoreStates Center after the 1995-96 season, the Phantoms moved in.

The expansion club was the city's first AHL franchise since the Firebirds, who played at the old Civic Center in University City from 1974 to '79.

Flyers legend Bill Barber, the Phantoms' first coach, led the team to the Calder Cup championship in 1998. John Stevens, who would coach Philadelphia to its second AHL title in 2005, was team captain for the inaugural championship club.

Wings

The spring of 1974 saw the greatest moment in Spectrum history when the Flyers won their first Stanley Cup. It was the only championship clinched at home by either the Flyers or Sixers, and the Wings' John Grant had a unique perspective.

Before the current incarnation of the Wings, there was an identically named lacrosse team that played at the Spectrum in 1974 and '75. The first home game for that Wings club was to be played the night of May 19, 1974. Earlier that day, the Flyers finished off the Bruins to win the Cup, making Grant's commute to the

Spectrum an adventure.

"It was one giant circle of a parade around the Spectrum," he was recalling recently from his home in Sudsbury, Ontario. "Cars were honking, people were drinking and partying."

It was a scene the Wings players would have joined in, except they had to work that night. Staying at a City Line Avenue Marriott, some players took cabs to the arena, but the closest the taxis could get was about a mile away, on the east end of Pattison Avenue. The players had no choice but to make their way through the revelers with equipment in hand.

"We were explaining what we were doing, walking around with sticks while everybody was partying. We thought nobody was coming to our game, they'd be too pie-eyed. But we had 16 or 17 thousand," says Grant, who had two goals in the Wings' 18-11 win over Montreal. "Every time our goalie [Wayne Platt] made a save, the crowd would chant 'Ber-nie, Ber-nie.' It was an amazing, amazing night."

The current version of the Wings began play in 1987 and have won six championships, the most recent in 2001. Grant returned to play for the Wings in 1987 and is the only player to suit up for both versions of the club.

It was not unusual, he says, to borrow some of the Flyers' equipment for a pickup hockey game or to shoot hoops with Doctor J.

"We were all like a family," he says.

Freedoms

The matriarch of that family, athletically anyway, would be tennis legend Billie Jean King, who played a number of times at the Spectrum and was a player-coach for the Philadelphia Freedoms tennis team in 1974.

King's remembrances range from the postcircus aroma that enveloped the facility to longtime guard Ed Minardi. She also told the story of a very famous head cheerleader.

"Elton John would come and sit on the bench and root us on," King says of her longtime friend. "He was just becoming big in the mid-'70s. One time he wanted to carry me out at a concert — shows you how thin we all were back then. He had me sing backup vocals one time and I told the engineer to turn off my mike."

John wrote the iconic song "Philadelphia Freedom" in honor of the team. The first time he played a demo of it for King was in a locker room in Denver. The nervous John told King, "If you don't like this, I'm toast."

According to John, the pounding drum beat behind the refrain "Phil-A-Delphia Freedom" represents King yelling at umpires.

The Kixx' Cesidio Colasante (right) and the Harrisburg Heat's David Barbosa in 2003. JENNIFER MIDBERRY / Daily News

Kixx

The Kixx proudly boast to being Philadelphia's longest continuous indoor soccer franchise. Forward Don D'Ambra and goalkeeper Peter Pappas have been with the club since it began play in 1996. D'Ambra, a product of North Catholic High School and Saint Joseph's University, has memories of the building that go back way before he became a professional.

"We played the State Cup championship on the [Spectrum] field when I was like 12 years old," he reflects. "We got our [butts] kicked. It wasn't a great memory in the end, but just being on the field was special."

D'Ambra has been a player-coach since 2002 and guided the Kixx to the 2007 championship. He will miss the old building.

"I want to get one of those crusty, old seats," he says with a chuckle. "Yeah, I want to get some memorabilia. I might just run around and start taking stuff to hang in the basement." S

Workers repair damage in February 1968 that made the Spectrum a pioneer in retractable roofs. RUSSELL SALMON / Inquirer

Raising the **Roof**

On Feb. 17, 1968, there were 11,000 people in the Spectrum to watch a performance of the Ice Capades. The way the newspapers reported it, many people thought they heard the sound of a low-flying airplane above the building. Instead, it was mostly tar paper being ripped from the roof.

Yes, it had blown off in 48 mph winds.

"It wasn't actually a hole," Ed Snider says. From the way it was described at the time, you could see sunlight shining through perforations in the metal roof in the area that was no longer covered by the tar paper. The damage was in an area 100 feet by 50 feet. The ice show was canceled that day, but not before the band calmed the patrons by playing, "Off We Go, Into the Wild, Blue Yonder."

Little did anyone know ...

The immediate answer — more tar paper — was applied. Three days later, the Sixers played an NBA doubleheader under the fixed roof, and then the Flyers played. Things seemed fine. But about a week after that, more roofing material blew off in three smaller areas — at which point the politicians got involved. Mayor James Tate, police commissioner Frank Rizzo, a bunch of other people and bunch of television cameras all climbed up ladders and inspected the roof. Tate ordered the building closed indefinitely.

There were revelations along the way that the Spectrum, still new, hadn't exactly received all of the required inspections before occupancy — at which point, District Attorney Arlen Specter became involved. There was talk of lie-detector tests for some officials, and political rivalries over this issue played out daily in the newspapers.

While the Sixers could play in Convention Hall and the Palestra, the Flyers had to play their "home" games in New York, Toronto and, mostly, Quebec City. Somehow, despite playing their final 14 games away from home, the Flyers still finished in first place in the NHL's West Division.

Twenty-seven days later, the Spectrum got its temporary occupancy permit.

— *Rich Hofmann*

On March 5, 2009, with temperatures hovering near the freezing point, the Harlem Globetrotters held court on the Spectrum's roof for an afternoon game against their familiar foes, the Washington Generals.

DAVID MAIALETTI / Daily News

Meadowlark Lemon makes a spectacle of himself during a Globetrotters visit in 1973. EARNEST S. EDDOWES / Inquirer

Roller Games star Judy Arnold. Spectrum archives

American Gladiators get some hang time at the Spectrum. Spectrum archives

Above, Carl Lewis (representing Houston) wins and Herschel Walker (left) comes in last in the 60-yard dash at the Philadelphia Track Classic on Jan. 23, 1981.

NORMAN Y. LONO / Daily News

George Mason University high jumper Scott Durham makes a crash landing at the 1981 Philadelphia Track Classic.

NORMAN Y. LONO / Daily News

World-renowned violinist Isaac Stern serenades Jimmy Connors after a win in 1978. ZOHRAB KAZANJIAN

Elton John's 'Philadelphia Freedom' was composed in honor of Billie Jean King's World Team Tennis franchise.

Spectrum archives

John McEnroe states his case to the umpire at the US Pro Tennis event in January 1979.
DENIS O'KEEFE / Daily News

Sgt. Slaughter (back to camera) shows Russian Nikolai Volkoff who's boss. MICHAEL MERCANTI / Daily News

Smackdown

The 10 wrestlers who competed the most at the Spectrum:

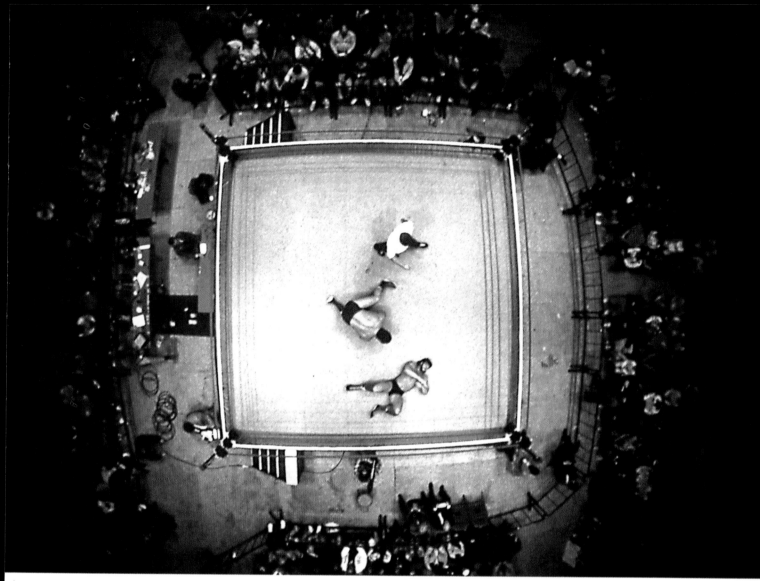

A pro wrestling match is seen from the unique perspective of the Spectrum's catwalk. SCOTT WEINER

Wrestling icon Bruno Sammartino (right) during one of his 45 matches at the Spectrum. SCOTT WEINER

Charlie Pauken drives 'Grave Digger' into the arena during a Monster Jam event Feb. 15, 2009. DAVID MAIALETTI / Daily News

Kumr the Hindu Faker lays on a bed of nails, assisted by two of the Spectrum's guards and Daily News writer Stan Hochman (in suit). ELWOOD P. SMITH / Daily News

Beau Bamburg does a split during a motocross event in January 2001.

CHARLES FOX / Daily News

Legendary daredevil Evel Knievel clears eight cars in this 1971 exhibition.

Gunther Gebel-Williams, of Ringling Bros. and Barnum & Bailey Circus, holds the Spectrum record with 221 appearances.

ED MAHAN

The Ice Capades arrived every year around the holidays for a different kind of fireworks show on skates.

ED MAHAN

Varying degrees of agility are displayed by circus performers, ranging from tightrope walkers (far right) to the elephants, whose march from the train station at 11th and Pattison to the Spectrum was always quite the attraction.

MICHAEL MERCANTI / Daily News

ED MAHAN

Jon Bon Jovi rocks the Spectrum with his Arena Football team, the Soul, during a 2004 pep rally. JOHN COSTELLO / Inquirer

Nathan Pitock, 8, of Villanova, shies away from a baby T-Rex, in town to hype the 'Walking with Dinosaurs' event in 2007. ALEJANDRO A. ALVAREZ / Daily News

Delimar Vera mingles with Sesame Street Live! characters in 2004. Vera had been in the news when she was reunited with her mother after a kidnapper led authorities to believe she had died in a fire in 1997. YONG KIM / Daily News

Nancy Kerrigan skates at the Spectrum in December 1993.

ED HILLE / Inquirer

Acknowledgments

THE *DAILY NEWS* WOULD LIKE TO THANK Comcast-Spectacor chairman Ed Snider and president Peter Luukko for approaching us to work as partners on this book. It has been a fun project on a building filled with countless memories.

No one worked harder on making this book possible than Ike Richman, the tireless vice president of public relations for Comcast-Spectacor. The institutional memory in that man's head is scary. We leaned heavily on the treasures unearthed by Comcast-Spectacor archives manager Brian McBride. Richman also introduced us to Roger Barone, who worked at the Spectrum for many years and used his unique access to capture many signature moments with excellent photographs.

And while the book is the product of the newsroom of the *Daily News*, especially our award-winning photo and sports departments, we did get a big hand from our colleagues at the *Inquirer*. There are several top-notch photos taken by the paper's talented staff over the years and editor Bill Marimow kindly allowed us to use the immense talents of the *Inquirer's* assistant managing editor for presentation, Kevin Burkett, on a freelance basis.

Thanks, too, to Carol Dooling and Susan DiIanni of the marketing department of Philadelphia Media Holdings, for their hustle and knowledge of the business of publishing a book, along with Edward Jutkowitz of Camino Publishing. Russell Peltz unlocked the vault to his vast collection of boxing records and Brenda Galloway-Wright and John Petit, of Temple's Paley Library, helped by finding historic photos from the university's Urban Archives. *Daily News* assistant sports editor Chuck Bausman also made many contributions.

Richman unfurled a host of people from Comcast-Spectacor who aided the project greatly. That list would include David James, Seth Kohler, Eric Nemeth, Larry Rubin, Lou Scheinfeld and Sarena Snider. Apologies — and our thanks — to anyone we may have overlooked in this listing.

Pat McLoone,
Managing editor,
Philadelphia Daily News

Like this rodeo horse, it's time for the Spectrum to take a bow.

Spectrum archives

Index